THE
INELIGIBLE
BACHELORETTE

The Ineligible Bachelorette
Taking a Hard Look at Why You Haven't Found "The One"
By Starr Burroughs

ISBN: 978-0-9985220-0-5 (POD) 978-0-9985220-1-2 (eBook)

Cover Design: Danijela Mijailovic
Editing Services: KathyIde.com
Publishing and Design Services: MelindaMartin.me

Printed in the United States of America.

THE
INELIGIBLE
BACHELORETTE

Taking a Hard Look at Why You Haven't Found "The One"

STARR BURROUGHS

Dedication

To the love of my life, Sean: You believed in me more than I did, pushed me to give my best, encouraged me when I felt like giving up, and stood by my side through it all. You've sacrificed much to help make my dreams a reality. Thank you for your unconditional love. I love you with my whole heart.

To my beautiful daughter, Brooklyn: Your sweetness and laughter bring joy to our lives. My prayer is that you will become a strong woman of God, following His purposes for your life.

Acknowledgments

I am the confident woman I am today because of my wonderful parents, Dave and Becky Franklin. I've always believed I could accomplish anything and move forward in life with a tenacious and driven spirit because of their upbringing. Thank you to my mother in-law, Debra Burroughs, for answering numerous questions and offering wisdom from her experiences as a self-published author. I would be lost without her guidance. Many thanks to my father in-law, Tim Burroughs, who continues to show me his support through his love and encouragement.

I couldn't have written this book without the expert help and advice from my editor, Kathy Ide. I prayed long before I began writing that I could find an exceptional editor, someone who could polish my content and make it the best it could be. After many deletions, additions, and much reorganizing, I am finally satisfied with the end product. Thank you to my friend Jennie Vatoseow, who has given many hours of her time—for free—to read, reread, and edit my original drafts. I relied on her for honest feedback throughout the writing process while she faithfully supported and encouraged me.

CONTENTS

"You are looking for someone who will not require or demand significant change. You are searching, therefore, for an ideal person—happy, healthy, interesting, content with life. Never before in history has there been a society filled with people so idealistic in what they are seeking in a spouse."

The Meaning of Marriage
by Timothy Keller with Kathy Keller

INTRODUCTION

DESTINATION: YOU

You're a single Christian woman waiting for God's best in all areas of life: career, family, marriage (not necessarily in that order). You're logical—you know you won't marry perfection, but is it too much to ask to find a man who genuinely loves Jesus, has a job, is socially normal, and has a decent body? I mean, come on.

But as you age, you begin to wonder, *Why aren't I married yet? What's wrong with me? Better yet, what's wrong with all the men out there? Can't they see how awesome I am? Why aren't they asking me out?*

You've no doubt received tons of advice from well-meaning friends, family, and even strangers. "It'll happen when you least expect it." "Make yourself more available." "Stop being so picky."

Well, I'll delve into some practical advice that goes way beyond those one-liners.

The purpose of this book is to take you on a journey. Destination: You. Why you choose the way you choose, why you're attracted to certain types of guys, what your fears are and why, and how you affect your relationships, or lack thereof.

I'm a thirty-something female who has learned a lot from her single life. As in, *Wow! My fears, my pride, and my expectations almost got in the way of my partnering with an amazing man and realizing a dream come true: a happy, healthy marriage.*

Fortunately, I did meet the love of my life, Sean.

Now, just because I'm married doesn't mean I'm oblivious to what today's generation is going through regarding the challenges of dating and marriage. I'm frustrated for singles who desperately want to get married but haven't found "the one" yet.

It feels as if we have little control over when or even if we will get married. How annoying. How frustrating. How confusing. Isn't marriage a gift from God? Doesn't He want us to get married? Shouldn't it be easier? I feel your pain.

I didn't go into my relationship with Sean thinking it was going to be happily ever after. I didn't know from the start that I was going to spend the rest of my life with him. God never specifically told me he would be my husband. There was never a "love at first sight" moment. And I spent the majority of our dating and engaged relationship dealing with my fears regarding marriage. Let's just say I'm not the romantic, idealistic type.

My prayer is that I can bring clarity and insight into this season of your life, shedding light on areas that require change in order for you to receive your breakthrough. I hope to offer gentle guidance by writing from the perspective of a married woman looking back on her single self, in addition to observations and conversations I've had with numerous singles and married couples. I want to help you have a realistic, objective view of your identity and truly love your authentic self. And, if needed, to adjust some of your expectations for a spouse in the same way I did.

Let the journey begin …

PART ONE

THE LAW OF ATTRACTION

Insecurity, pride, and fear play an enormous role in the types of people we're interested in. Often our attractions lead us to the wrong type of person over and over again, or we're so picky that we're never drawn to anyone. If you have yet to find the right fit, it's possible you're too insecure, proud, or fearful to be with someone who could be "the one."

As you read this section, you'll learn why you're drawn to certain people. The basis of your attractions will be challenged and you'll finish with a greater ability to discern whether they come from a place of insecurity, pride, or fear.

CHAPTER 1

THE DRIVING FORCE OF INSECURITY

In high school, a friend of mine had a serious girlfriend (as serious as a teenage relationship can be) who went to another school. This girl seemed perfect for him. And yet he cheated on her constantly.

As I got older, I heard shocking stories about well-known pastors and evangelists who were caught in affairs, which ended their marriages and ministries. How could godly men who proclaimed the message of the gospel allow this to happen? And how could any man stay faithful if these apparently great men of God couldn't? This worry created an insecurity inside me that affected my relationship with Sean, the man I eventually married.

Even though no boyfriend of mine had ever cheated on me (that I knew of), I still lacked trust. This was not based on any character flaw of Sean's, but on my own insecurity. I didn't want to be the naïve girl who didn't believe her husband could be unfaithful. So my tendency was to jump to the other end of the spectrum. I believed the worst so I wouldn't be taken for a fool by believing the best.

In the beginning of our relationship, if Sean talked to a girl for too long, or seemed too friendly with a woman from work, or didn't give me enough attention, I felt unsure about the health of our relationship. My insecurity caused me to think irrationally.

In an attempt to overcome my uncertainties, I decided to communicate how I was feeling to Sean, and he was gracious enough to be sensitive to my concerns.

He steered clear of situations that would cause me to feel worried about his commitment to me. Yet I couldn't make Sean a prisoner to my feelings. I had to do what I could to mature and move beyond this worry. So I evaluated my thoughts to determine if they were coming from a place of insecurity or reality.

I BELIEVED THE WORST SO I WOULDN'T BE TAKEN FOR A FOOL BY BELIEVING THE BEST.

There was nothing he could've done to make me trust him more. He was already attentive, considerate, and full of character. There wasn't even a hint of inappropriate behavior between him and another woman. Over time, my belief that he wouldn't cheat on me grew stronger.

Maybe you've had a similar insecurity that has negatively affected, or even ruined, a good relationship. The driving force of that insecurity has shaped who you will or won't date and has manifested itself in your relationships, or lack thereof. Take a moment to think about what has happened in your past that may be holding you back today.

Those experiences don't have to hinder you in the dating world. In the same way I was able to overcome my insecurity, you can overcome yours. By becoming aware of what those insecurities are, communicating them to a mentor or significant other, and praying about them, you'll be able to move past them and enjoy a healthy relationship.

Let's take a look at how insecurity influences women by analyzing these hypothetical situations based on real-life events:

Sally was never popular in high school. She felt insecure whenever she was with a guy who didn't have a lot of friends surrounding him. Wanting to guarantee a social status that she couldn't achieve on her own, Sally never felt attracted to anyone who wasn't among the "socially elite."

Robin lacked vision and ambition. So she felt insecure whenever she was with a guy who couldn't provide her with that. Since she didn't know how to be successful on her own, the only way she could be happy in a relationship was if she was with someone who was already established in his career.

Colleen only dated men who were charismatic leaders. She thought CEO-type men were better than others. Since she considered them to be the best of the best, Colleen was too insecure to be associated with, or attracted to, anyone she deemed "less than."

These girls don't realize that their insecurities are the leading factor behind their choosing and responding process when it comes to deciding whether or not they are interested in someone. Their insecurities have determined their attractions.

When you're insecure, it can be a long, difficult process to find a special someone to spend the rest of your life with. If you lack confidence, you'll find it hard to "put yourself out there," to go to parties, to be more social, to make yourself more attractive. You're always wondering, *What's the point in trying? No one is going to like me anyway.*

Insecure people feel a need to be connected to certain types of people who make them feel more secure. There's nothing wrong with feeling secure. But if you're depending on someone else to provide you with confidence so you can feel good about yourself, you'll always be looking for the same type of guy: the one you're convinced is going to give you the life you've always wanted, the one who's "better" than all the other guys, the one who will boost your ego.

To some extent, we're all insecure. Have you ever thought, *I wonder what people will think when they see me with him?* Or imagined how cool you're going to look in front of your friends because this incredibly hot, successful guy likes you? If so, you're insecure.

My goal is not to keep you from wondering what others will think about you based on the person you're with. Instead, I want to keep you from making decisions about who you will or won't date based on what others might think about you.

If friends and family have accused you of being too picky, if you aren't dating and don't have any pursuers, if you have a nonnegotiables list a mile long and no one seems to fit your qualifications, it's time to ask yourself if your attractions are rooted in insecurity. To find out, look for these five patterns:

Pattern #1

You always like the guy who makes you look good or causes others to be jealous. He's the type everyone else wants. Your view of yourself is the leading factor behind your attraction to him. Ultimately, you're choosing him out of your own selfish motivation.

Pattern #2

You like yourself better when you're dating. You have a greater sense of self-worth when you're connected to a man. A romantic relationship brings security and meaning to your life.

Pattern #3

You always like guys who have something you lack. The missing pieces from your life—such as financial security, a present father, a whole family unit, or popularity—have created an insecurity in you that draws you to the type of man who can seemingly heal your wounds.

Pattern #4

You're afraid to show interest in someone. You never initiate a date, converse with someone you might be interested in, or befriend a potential significant other. It's not that you're choosing a certain type of person as a result of your insecurities. You're too insecure to choose anyone at all.

Pattern #5

You're consistently attracted to the wrong type. Your insecurities have led you to a certain kind of man over and over again, but you never have success with him. Either the feelings aren't reciprocated because you aren't his type, or the relationship simply never works out.

Once you start to see a pattern in your attractions, you can honestly evaluate what you are or aren't drawn to in a potential spouse. You will be open to more types of men because you'll be aware of any insecurity that is influencing your interest in the opposite sex. And you'll take risks and do what needs to be done in order to move forward in a potential relationship.

ATTRACTIONS ROOTED IN SECURITY

When you accept yourself, like yourself, and are proud of who you are, in spite of your shortcomings, you'll become more secure.

So, how do you move beyond your insecurities? Surround yourself with confident people who believe in you and support you. Find a church you love, attend a small group, and let their encouragement help you gain confidence.

As your understanding of Jesus and His love for you grows, your love for yourself will grow. You'll begin to compare less because you are more satisfied with who you are.

Secure people have a larger pool of prospective spouses to choose from because their confidence is not dependent on their significant others. You can be attracted to someone who may not meet socially acceptable standards, someone who's not taller than you, someone who doesn't have a lot of money, or who isn't very attractive or charismatic or connected to the right family, or a leader of leaders. You won't care what others will think of you based on the person you're with.

Your confidence will be internal, allowing you to function as a whole person rather than a wounded one. Wounded people need someone in their lives who has the ability to heal those wounds and the resulting insecurities. It is God's job to do that.

Wounded people attract other wounded people. So if you want to attract a healthy and whole man, you must be a healthy and whole woman.

If you've come to realize that you have insecurities that are driving your attractions for the opposite sex, it's time to begin the healing process. Ask God to make you aware of the insecurities that are keeping you from finding a great partner. Ask Him to show you how to overcome them. Pray that He will guide you to the right person to help heal those wounds. And keep in mind, that person may not be your significant other.

God's desire is for us to be confident and secure in who He has created us to be. Trust in God as your source, not in a man. Through Him, you will have the freedom that comes with confidently accepting who you are.

CHAPTER 2

THE DRIVING FORCE
OF PRIDE

Pride can influence our attractions and hinder us from falling in love with the right person. Unfortunately, proud people don't realize they could be missing out on an opportunity with an amazing individual because they're blinded by their own greatness.

Jennifer was only interested in men who added to her already impressive resume. She expected a potential dating partner to be just as successful as she was, if not more so. And she would never consider someone who wasn't. Pride in her accomplishments caused her to view herself as better than others.

No matter how hard Monica tried, she could never be attracted to a man who had asked out other girls in her social sphere before her, especially one of her friends. It crushed her ego to know she wasn't his first choice.

Rebecca was proud of who she had become and was waiting for God's best. What she didn't realize is that she was defining what the best was for her instead of letting God do that. Her pride kept her from being attracted to a man who didn't fit the fantasy image she had in her head.

My Pride

I tend to be a proud person. I don't want to appear weak or needy. I'm also a perfectionist, so I expect a lot from myself and from others. I know perfection isn't achievable, but I think everyone should always work toward excellence. (Isn't that what all perfectionists think?) But this way of thinking is exhausting. It puts a lot of pressure on yourself and others. In fact, it negatively affected my relationship with Sean when we dated.

The underlying expectation I had for myself to be excellent in everything spilled over into my view of Sean. I wanted him to put as much effort and discipline into taking care of his physical appearance as I did. I couldn't understand why he didn't have that same goal for himself. So I had a critical attitude toward him. Ultimately, my pride in this area influenced my attraction to him.

Having pride in my physical appearance wasn't bad. But I let it determine my attractions for the opposite sex. I second-guessed my feelings for Sean because he didn't have the "perfect" physique. According to my standards, he wasn't good enough for me in this particular area.

Unfortunately, proud people don't realize they can be missing out on an opportunity with an amazing individual because they're blinded by their own greatness.

I deserved someone who excelled in physical fitness … or so I told myself. What I didn't realize is that I prioritized this in my search for a significant other. If a man didn't meet that qualification, I wasn't attracted to him. And since Sean wasn't as fit as I wanted him to be, it took a while for me to allow myself to become interested in him as more than a friend.

IF YOU'RE LOOKING FOR A SPOUSE WHO IS YOUR EQUAL IN ALL AREAS, PRIDE WILL TURN YOUR HEART TOWARD PEOPLE WHO FIT THE QUALIFICATIONS YOU'VE DEFINED INSTEAD OF WHO GOD THINKS YOU SHOULD BE WITH.

At the time, I didn't understand that my attraction for Sean would go much deeper than outward appearance. I wish I could've told my single self that genuine love can cause you to be attracted to the person you're with. And that I would care far more about the character of the man I married, and his love for Jesus and for me, than I would about his body. Then maybe I wouldn't have made my decisions to be with someone based on such a superficial standard.

I almost turned my back on Sean because he wasn't as fit as I wanted him to be. Ridiculous, right? But women often do this without realizing it.

If you're looking for a spouse who is your equal in all areas, pride will turn your heart toward people who fit the qualifications you've defined instead of who God thinks you should be with.

If what you're looking for in a spouse is mutual love for a lifetime, you may need to lay aside your pride and make compromises in areas that you've given priority to. Don't lower your required standards, such as godly character and a man's love for you and commitment to you. But be willing to negotiate in areas you feel you deserve your "equal" in.

Once you admit that pride is negatively influencing your attractions, repent for the sin of judging others. Spend time in prayer, because Jesus' love will enable you to love other people better. This will result in fewer judgments and comparisons, allowing you to more accurately see the worth of individuals. It's hard to reject people based on pride when you have the love of Jesus inside you for them.

How do you know if your pride is tainting your judgment of others and influencing your attractions? There are two signs to look for within yourself so you can determine whether your attractions are rooted in pride.

A SUPERIORITY COMPLEX

It's important to find the right balance between being proud of yourself and your accomplishments and thinking more highly of yourself than you ought.

Paul says in Romans 12:3, "Because of the privilege and authority God has given me, I give each of you this warning: Don't think you are better than you really are. Be honest in your evaluation of yourselves, measuring yourselves by the faith God has given us."

We should do things that cause us to feel confident, yet hold those accomplishments loosely, not allowing them to make us feel like we're better than others. Otherwise, we can develop a superiority complex that will keep any man from qualifying as "good enough."

Proud women think they deserve the best of the best. Ironically, this keeps them from being attractive to most men, even those who are as successful as they are. They will make men feel inferior, and who wants to be around someone like that? Only an insecure person with low self-esteem would take that kind of punishment.

A woman may not recognize that she has a superiority complex, but it's obvious to others based on her actions. She only gives her time and attention to the man she considers to be above the rest. She won't even look twice at a guy who doesn't appear to have any special qualities about him, such as popularity or wealth. Maybe she is great. Maybe she has accomplished many things. Maybe she is incredibly attractive. But that doesn't mean every man out there is beneath her.

Women with an inflated ego are always waiting for someone to come along who is more talented, more charismatic, more intelligent than their current options. They compare their own physical appearance, their friends, their family, and their money against a potential boyfriend and come to the conclusion that they can do better. Because of their accomplishments and successes, they believe they deserve someone who has done as much as they have, if not more. Their ego would take a hit if they dated someone who didn't meet all of their qualifications.

When you're more concerned with how others perceive you than you are with allowing your heart to be attracted to a flawed individual, your attractions are likely rooted in pride. You'll constantly be stuck in this vicious cycle of waiting for someone better. Your pride inflates your ego, which in turn inflates your expectations, and you'll be kept in the waiting game for way too long. This mind-set is selfish and inaccurate.

A FRAGILE EGO

A woman's ego can be crushed if she feels like a number on a man's list of conquests. She may never be attracted to that man, even if he's a good one. It's incredibly unappealing when a man makes a woman feel like second (or third or fourth) best. No one wants to feel like leftovers. Every girl desires to be pursued and made to feel like a queen worthy of that pursuit.

A woman may not care to date a man who has asked out other girls before her—especially those in her social circle, or even her friends. Unfortunately, it's rare that a man will marry the only woman he's pursued. The guy you consider to be a potential mate may have loved someone else before you. He might have even been engaged. So what if you weren't his first option?

Sometimes women force men into a lose-lose situation. If they ask too many girls out, they are excommunicated from the eligible bachelor pool and no girl will give them a chance. But if they don't ask any girls out, they are talked about behind their backs and not respected because girls think they aren't assertive enough.

So what's the perfect balance? Asking only a few girls out? Spreading out the dates so as not to draw attention to themselves and who they're pursuing? What an impossible situation we put men in. How could they ever get it right?

Okay, so it's probably not a good idea to ask out a girl's six best friends and when they all say no, pursue the last girl standing. But women can't expect a man to never have dated, liked, or asked out any of her friends, especially if they have mutual acquaintances. It's not realistic.

Single men are in the process of figuring out who they want to spend the rest of their lives with, just like you are. This requires a man to befriend and date other girls. So don't expect to be his "one and only" until after you're married.

Use your judgment, intuition, and discernment when considering a potential boyfriend who has dated other girls. Does he seem like a player or a good guy who's just trying to figure this dating thing out? If he's a quality guy you could be interested in, give him a chance. Don't say no just because he's asked out other girls before you.

THE GOOD SIDE OF PRIDE

Having pride in who you are doesn't have to lead to an inflated ego. When used correctly, confidence can be very attractive. Self-assured women know their worth, what they want, and what type of man is special enough for them. They have standards, but they hold those standards with an open hand, allowing the Holy Spirit to speak to them and alter their expectations if needed. They can respect and value a man even if he isn't right for them.

When you recognize the worth of people, you won't look down on them or view them as less than you are.

CHAPTER 3

THE DRIVING FORCE
OF FEAR

Sarah grew up in a divorced home, and most of her family members didn't know Jesus. She came up with a list of standards for a husband that came out of her fear of re-creating her family history. Her most important criteria was that he come from a family of strong Christians. She figured that such a man would know how to be a good husband and father and would not make the same mistakes her dad made.

In spite of her list, Sarah fell in love with a man whose parents had separated when he was young, and the majority of his family members were not Christians. His mother and father had already passed away, so he didn't have the strong family unit she hoped for.

Sarah could've walked away from this man because he didn't meet her qualifications for a spouse. But she realized these standards came from her fears, not God, so she chose faith and love. God brought together these two imperfect people, with their tragedies, struggles, and disappointments.

The only reason Sarah was able to recognize him as a potential spouse was that she made the decision to submit her fears to God. Eventually, they got married, recently had their first child, and are now building a thriving Christian family together.

Fear keeps us from accomplishing our dreams and living life to the fullest. It can be all encompassing, overpowering, and debilitating.

How has fear affected your relationships? Are you so afraid of marrying someone like your dad that you're instantly turned off by anyone who has similar traits? Are you afraid of marrying someone who has a successful but demanding career because one of your parents was constantly at work and absent from the home? Are you afraid of marrying someone who is really attractive because you think he'll have more opportunities to cheat?

Are you overly cautious about the type of person you're willing to marry because you're terrified of repeating the same mistakes you saw or experienced growing up? Have you created a wall around your heart that keeps pain out but also holds love at bay?

I didn't think I was a fearful person. I've gone skydiving and bungee jumping. I like speaking in front of people and making new friends. I'm not concerned about what people think of me. And I'm not worried that bad things are going to happen. But three major fears plagued my single life and influenced my relationship with Sean. These fears were buried so deep down that only a promising relationship with a great man brought them out. Then it was like a volcano of fears exploded all at once.

Maybe you'll recognize yourself in one of these fears.

1. THE FEAR OF CHOOSING THE WRONG PERSON

I was worried that if I allowed myself to fall in love with the wrong person, I'd marry him and my life would be doomed. I didn't really believe that there was only one person in the world for me. But that's how I acted.

I ignored my emotions because I was convinced they would lead me astray. Instead I let logic reign. I thought I was protecting myself from making the wrong decision, but in reality, I couldn't fall in love because I wasn't listening to my heart.

I knew it was up to God to bring the right person to me, but I was still terrified I'd somehow screw it up. Since I preferred staying single to marrying the wrong man, I picked apart nearly everything about Sean. Every little flaw he had signaled that our relationship was destined for failure.

Sean never put his dishes into the dishwasher, even though it would only take a few seconds, and I wasn't shy about informing him of that fact. He loved to cuddle and watch TV, even when there were tasks that needed to be marked off the to-do list. I criticized him for relaxing too much. And when he said things like "You're more beautiful than the most beautiful sunset," I considered his compliments too over the top to believe.

My fears kept me in control. They prevented me from being attracted to the person who had attributes I was afraid to deal with. I thought if I held on to those worries, my attractions would lead me away from the wrong person and toward the right person.

But my fears were deceiving because none of Sean's "flaws" were worth breaking up over. I had magnified them in my mind because I was subconsciously trying to sabotage our relationship. I liked Sean a lot. I wanted to be around him all the time. I enjoyed talking to him. I smiled and laughed when we were together. I loved holding his hand, kissing him, and snuggling with him. I loved that he adored me. But I didn't know what to do with the romantic emotions I was feeling. I was in a state of confusion because these feelings of love coexisted with feelings of doubt and fear.

2. THE FEAR OF SETTLING FOR LESS THAN BEST

In the beginning of my relationship with Sean, I wondered if God had someone better for me than him. I knew "better" didn't mean that someone else might have more worth than Sean, but that there was someone out there who had all of the good qualities Sean had plus more. Someone who was more attractive, more financially secure, more established, had better connections.

Over time, I realized that plenty of men were "better" than Sean. And plenty of women were better than me. There will always be someone out there who possesses more impressive qualities than you and the person you're with.

> ## THERE WILL ALWAYS BE SOMEONE OUT THERE WHO POSSESSES MORE IMPRESSIVE QUALITIES THAN YOU AND THE PERSON YOU'RE WITH.

If our hearts are submitted to God, He won't let us settle for less than the best. That doesn't mean the road ahead will never be bumpy. But when we trust in God to help us make the right choices, He will bring our fears and insecurities to the surface so that we can overcome them. And He will purify our desires to match His. Those godly desires will lead us to respond to and choose the right mates for us.

3. THE FEAR THAT MARRIAGE GETS WORSE WITH TIME

To me, marriage was a depreciating investment, like driving a brand-new car off the lot. I thought that all couples grew apart.

Isn't that what society tells us? How many sitcoms and reality shows are about fighting couples who lie and cheat and spend time with anyone besides their spouses? When we see that type of scenario played out as entertainment, we internalize the message, eventually believing that what we see on TV is what happens in real life.

This current fatherless generation has seen marriages fall apart due to affairs, selfishness, pride, dishonesty, and sometimes for no other reason than Mom and Dad "fell out of love." They have concluded that they can get everything they need from a committed relationship— sex, companionship, romance, and love—outside of marriage. So who in their right mind would want to get married if a divorce seems inevitable?

Though I didn't agree with this thought process, I was still afraid there was some truth to it. So I worried that Sean and I wouldn't be able to keep ourselves from drifting apart.

FEAR KEPT ME FROM LOVE AND MARRIAGE

Fear paralyzed me and controlled my mind and heart. It tainted my perspective. I figured I only had one shot to make marriage work, and I couldn't stand the thought of blowing it.

I hoped, in the end, I would find true and lasting love. But I was terrified to take the first step down that road. I felt as though I were in a parked car, wanting to go somewhere great but too afraid to put the car in drive and my foot on the gas pedal. I believed there was someone out there for me, but fear of failure, fear of love, and fear of intimacy kept me from stepping into the unknown realm of love.

I acted as if failure was guaranteed. But it never was. It was simply feared.

If you live your life with the fear of making the wrong decision regarding whom you should marry, you'll never be able to date with peace. And you won't allow your heart to open up to a potential spouse. You won't be open to anyone who doesn't fit the image you have in your head.

Growing up in the church, I was taught that it's damaging to date a lot of people. The goal was to date with the sole purpose of marriage in mind. If you married the one and only person you ever went out with, that was the ideal scenario. But when my friends who dated with this mentality broke up, they felt shame and embarrassment, which then demotivated them from dating at all.

I ACTED AS IF FAILURE WAS GUARANTEED. BUT IT NEVER WAS. IT WAS SIMPLY FEARED.

Love and the pursuit of love is anything but quick and efficient. It's laden with mistakes and failures, trial and error. I'm not saying you'll marry the wrong person. But it's likely you'll make some mistakes on the path toward marriage.

If you wait for God to speak before saying yes to going on a date, you will probably never date. Of course it's important to seek God's leading in this area. But when you accept that the process can be messy, and that every mishap isn't a sign from God that you should break up, it'll be easier to make decisions when it comes to who you should or shouldn't go out with and eventually marry.

THE RECIPE FOR SUCCESS: ALMOST PERFECT

People who are afraid of failure aim for perfection in a potential mate, thinking that will guarantee them marital success. They Build-a-Husband in their minds, picking out all the looks, qualities, and attributes they desire. The problem is that it's extremely difficult to find a real-life husband who is equal to what we've imagined.

Anyone you partner up with will come with his own set of issues. You may never find someone who precisely matches the Build-a-Husband you've created. Even if you find someone who's close to being the man of your dreams, he will likely be different from your ideal image.

Yet we still think that if we find someone who meets the vast majority of our qualifications, it's likely the relationship will work out. After all, employers make their decisions on hiring new employees based on how qualified the candidates are, believing that will bring the company success. We date in much the same way.

But if your qualifications are based on fear, you've created an inaccurate job description. That's why you're getting all the wrong applicants. And why you never seem to be attracted to the right person.

Your recipe for success has become a recipe for singleness.

How can you be sure your qualifications list isn't derived from your fears? Well, first you have to understand why you are or aren't attracted to particular individuals.

Think of a person you're attracted to and write down why. What is it about him that you're drawn to? Now think of someone you aren't attracted to romantically. Why aren't you interested in him as more than a friend? What is it about him that is unappealing to you? If you're honest with your answers, you'll be able to determine whether your attractions are motivated by fear.

Maybe he's an athlete and you're afraid he won't be able to spend enough time with you or your future kids. Maybe he doesn't serve in the church as much as you do, and you're afraid that means he won't ever be the spiritual leader in your home.

You start noticing a pattern. You're never attracted to the men who like you and are available to you. You're attracted to unreachable men—maybe they're famous, or married, or non-Christians, or guys who will never be in your social sphere. Maybe you're more attracted to your fantasy man than to the options you have in real life.

After analyzing your attractions, you realize that your fear of commitment has been the driving force all along!

You can only protect yourself behind your shelter of fears for so long. At some point you will have to deal with them if you want to move forward in a relationship with an imperfect man.

The good news is, your fears can be overcome. And the potential of love is worth the risk of failure.

HOW TO OVERCOME: SEEK THE SPIRIT

Even after Sean professed his love for me, I still wasn't sure if I loved him. I didn't even know what romantic love was supposed to feel like. I saw couples walk hand-in-hand, fingers intertwined, arms around each other with a lovey-dovey look in their eyes. I just didn't get it.

I viewed love as both fascinating and foreign. It was hard for me to imagine loving the same person forever. I couldn't wrap my mind around the idea of actually wanting to be with my husband all the time. Or enjoying being with him more than I enjoyed being alone or with my closest girlfriend. Or him loving me as much as I loved him.

Love was an elusive idea to me, and I couldn't quite grasp the power and pull of it. I didn't know how to deal with the fact that I could be making a lifelong commitment to Sean. And I sure didn't trust my heart.

Because my fears and uncertainties clouded my judgment, it took a long time for me to discern why I lacked peace in my relationship with Sean. So one night

I sat in my bed, begging God to give me a clear yes or no when it came to dating him. I had already received a yes from everyone around me. My family loved Sean, my friends loved him, and my pastors loved us together. But I hadn't heard a clear yes from the most important source: God. I vowed not to fall asleep until I heard from Him.

After praying for what felt like hours, my high aspirations of an all-night prayer meeting fell short at 1 a.m., when I fell asleep. But the next morning I knew in my spirit that fear was the only reason I would have for breaking up with Sean. I also knew I wasn't about to make such a big decision that wasn't based on faith!

I discussed my fears with Sean so he could understand what was going on inside me, pray with me, and stand in faith with me. When I communicated my worries out loud, they lost power over me. They suddenly didn't seem so realistic after all. I knew God would guide me in the right direction because I constantly sought Him in prayer and asked for wisdom and guidance (Proverbs 3:5–6). And as stated in Psalm 32:8, "The Lord says, 'I will guide you along the best pathway for your life. I will advise you and watch over you.'" Through prayer and the support of Sean, I submitted my fears to the Holy Spirit. And in time I became more faith-filled than fear-filled.

HOW TO OVERCOME: FOCUS ON THE GOOD

In order to move forward in my relationship with Sean, I had to recognize what a great guy I had right in front of me. Sean respected me, believed in me, and wholeheartedly loved me. He empowered me, was never intimidated or threatened by me, always saw the best in me, and was the most amazing human example of God's love for me. He treated me like a queen, treasured me, listened to me, valued my opinion, loved serving me, gave me his attention, enjoyed spending time with me, and simply adored me. What a lucky girl I was!

One evening, as we were saying good night, he began prophesying over me. He told me that he could see me writing books and becoming a great influencer. He told me I'd change the world. He wanted to support my dreams and help make them a reality. He spoke constant words of encouragement over me, complimented me often, and always communicated his love for me. He saw us as partners.

I'd prayed long ago that God would give me a man who would love me the way He loved the church, as described in Ephesians 5:25. I wanted to be with someone I would feel comfortable giving my heart to. And I wanted to be with someone who could love me the way Jesus loved me but in human form. Eventually I realized that Jesus had sent this man to me because of his relentless, unconditional love for me.

HOW TO OVERCOME: SHIFT YOUR PERSPECTIVE

I used to envy people who had a picture-perfect image of marriage in their heads, because they expected the best instead of fearing the worst. It seemed easier for them to fall in love because they viewed marriage as "happily ever after," living day in and day out with their best friend, having beautiful children together, and enjoying wonderful companionship for the rest of their lives. Since I couldn't believe for the best, I prepared myself for the worst—believing that marriage would bring only negative things.

But Sean had a beautiful image of marriage in his mind. He loved the idea of spending a lifetime with his best friend. He believed that our love for each other would get stronger over time. He imagined us growing closer and closer to each other. He believed we'd raise children who loved us and loved Jesus. He thought life would be better as a married man than as a single guy, and he couldn't wait to get hitched.

His perspective helped me think more positively about marriage. I began to see what he saw and believe for the best instead of expecting the worst. God used Sean to increase my faith, which in turn made me more excited about marriage. I'm glad God responds to our faith, even if it is as small as a mustard seed (Luke 17:6).

HOW TO OVERCOME: ACCEPT THE RISK

It wasn't willpower or desperation that helped me move past my fears. It was the understanding that marriage is a risk and that I was with a man who was worth that risk. Still, I desperately wanted to make the right decision.

I wanted to know the end of our story. I wanted a guarantee that everything would work out, that we would never get divorced, that he wouldn't cheat on me, that he would always love me unconditionally and pursue me. That who he was when we were dating would be who he was after we got married. That he would be a great father. That he would always love Jesus and always adore me. But I never got that guarantee.

I had to take a step of faith—no, a giant leap—and trust that it would all work out. I had to believe that God was guiding me and that my feelings for Sean were not leading me astray.

One day, I was browsing online and came across an article that I knew God put there just for me. The author wrote that marriage isn't just about settling down. It's an adventure she had the privilege of going on with her husband. She compared it to standing at the edge of a cliff, hand-in-hand with her love, and jumping. Terrified, but happy.

That short article spoke hope into all the areas where I was feeling anxious and fearful in my relationship with Sean. It gave me a picture of what an amazing adventure marriage could be. So I printed it out and put it in my wallet, and whenever I needed a little reminder that marriage was a leap of faith, I took it out and gave it a quick read.

I knew, at some point in the future, I'd have to jump. But I hated the thought. I don't mind taking calculated risks, as in "If I fail, it'll be okay." But it wouldn't be okay if I failed in marriage. I wanted to be married to the same person forever. I needed to trust God, Sean, and myself, and believe that jumping off that cliff was the right thing to do. I had to do it afraid.

PART TWO

HOW THE LAW OF ATTRACTION PLAYS OUT IN YOUR LIFE

When the Law of Attraction influences your relationships, you'll have the tendency to overlook great, godly options for mates and remain confused as to why you still haven't found anyone yet. If insecurity, pride, or fear is the driving force behind your interest in the opposite sex (or lack thereof), your standards will be misguided and the process for finding the right person will be hindered.

After reading this section, your expectations for a mate will get back on track and in line with God's qualifications for your future spouse. You'll also be in a better position to spot common pitfalls in the judging process prior to deciding whether you want to date someone.

CHAPTER 4

FROM SHEPHERD TO KING

Poor David. He was a shepherd, an underdog, a nobody. Overlooked even by his own father. But he had no idea his life was about to change forever.

God told the prophet Samuel to go to Bethlehem to anoint the new king. He invited Jesse, David's father, and his sons, as well as the elders of the town to join him for a sacrifice.

> When they arrived, Samuel took one look at Eliab and thought, "Surely this is the Lord's anointed!"
>
> But the Lord said to Samuel, "Don't judge by his appearance or height, for I have rejected him. The Lord doesn't see things the way you see them. People judge by outward appearance, but the Lord looks at the heart."
>
> Then Jesse told his son Abinadab to step forward and walk in front of Samuel. But Samuel said, "This is not the one the Lord

has chosen." Next Jesse summoned Shimea, but Samuel said, "Neither is this the one the Lord has chosen." In the same way all seven of Jesse's sons were presented to Samuel. But Samuel said to Jesse, "The Lord has not chosen any of these." Then Samuel asked, "Are these all the sons you have?"

"There is still the youngest," Jesse replied. "But he's out in the fields watching the sheep and goats."

"Send for him at once," Samuel said. "We will not sit down to eat until he arrives."

So Jesse sent for him. He was dark and handsome, with beautiful eyes.

And the Lord said, "This is the one; anoint him."

So as David stood there among his brothers, Samuel took the flask of olive oil he had brought and anointed David with the oil. And the Spirit of the Lord came powerfully upon David from that day on. Then Samuel returned to Ramah. (1 Samuel 16:6–13)

David was an average, unimpressive guy who hadn't done anything noteworthy. Ironically, we sometimes treat prospective men the same way Samuel treated Jesse's sons.

What is it about the shepherd type of guy that is so unappealing, so unattractive, that you think, *I know he's not right for me, so I won't even include him in the lineup?*

HE SHOWED ME THAT AS LONG AS I WAS OKAY WITH A SHEPHERD BOY, HE WOULD BRING ME A MAN ANOINTED TO BE KING.

When I was single, I was looking for a king. Someone who met all of society's standards. Someone who had accomplished many things, had made money, was settled in life, and had exceeded my own level of success.

But this passage altered my view on how to choose a spouse. God revealed to me that I should be looking for a shepherd. Someone He approved of, who met the godly standards He had given to me, and who was rich in godly character. He showed me that as long as I was okay with a shepherd boy, he would bring me a man anointed to be king.

But I knew if the prophet Samuel almost chose incorrectly, so could I. After all, Samuel was familiar with the voice of God and had clear direction on where to go and whom to anoint. But even he didn't get it right immediately. After one glance at Eliab, Samuel was convinced he was going to be the new king. When the Lord nixed Eliab, Samuel had to go through the entire lineup of brothers.

I wondered, was I really a better judge of character than this prophet of God?

What about you? Are you a better judge of character than Samuel? Probably not.

So, what can we do to discern who the "shepherds" among us are? First, we need to avoid judging a book by its cover. And second, we have to let God lead.

JUDGING A BOOK BY ITS COVER

One evening I went to a girls' night at a friend's house. We were celebrating because my friend had recently bought a new condo and remodeled it. Our hostess was great at befriending men. She wasn't at all intimidated by them. She was fun to be around, and she was attractive.

As we were eating and chatting, a couple of her male neighbors knocked on the door. These guys had helped her move in and also assisted with some of the remodeling. She invited them in and they began chatting with all of us.

Every girl there, besides me, was single. The two guys acted like they'd hit the jackpot—entering a room full of single women they couldn't wait to impress. They were both very friendly, and one of them in particular worked the room, trying to make everyone laugh.

When he got to my table, he started chatting with us. But all the other girls ignored him, talking to each other, barely acknowledging the only male in their presence. They had apparently already determined that he was not an option for them.

I carried on a wonderful conversation with the charming man that my single girlfriends ignored.

When you're in your teens and twenties, you tend to judge quickly. After reading the first few pages of a book, you decide it's not worth your time, so you stop reading.

Unfortunately, that's how I treated Sean. He made a great first impression, with his gorgeous green eyes! But it was months before I was willing to read past the first couple of pages to get to know him better. It was obvious he was a "shepherd" who hadn't begun walking in his "kingly" role. He wasn't established in his business yet, not making a lot of money, not settled in a lucrative career. But he was funny, easy to talk to, kind, and I enjoyed being around him.

In time, I learned that he was a man of character who loved Jesus and ministry. But his "shepherdly" qualities weren't impressive enough for me.

When I talked to my mom about this new guy in my life, she reminded me what was most important in a relationship. She was more swayed by the fact that he was a godly man of integrity than the kingly attributes I was impressed by, like looks, career, and finances.

It took me a while, but eventually, I listened to her.

Maybe you also have a track record of judging too quickly. If the men you know don't have the vision and ambition you crave, the looks you desire, and the charisma you feel you need, you immediately think there's no chemistry, no connection, and therefore, no future.

Yet I'll bet you've been overlooked or judged yourself from time to time. Maybe when some guy learned about your colored past, he quickly began showing interest in someone else. Or someone dumped you because you weren't as attractive as another girl or because you don't come from a healthy, wealthy family. It's easy to overlook others when there's an Eliab in the room.

Let's say you meet a guy who is a rock-star Christian. At least he dresses and sings like one. Or maybe he's a pastor.

Or a business leader. The lead usher at your church. It seems obvious that he's anointed by God. But is he right for you?

The most obvious choice isn't always the right one.

Even Jesus was judged to be a nobody. He was a carpenter, born in a manger. He wasn't rich or from a family of status. People couldn't accept that He was someone great because He was just too ... normal.

If you don't want to be the kind of person who hastily judges others, stay open-minded about the type of man God has for you. This will allow you to be attracted to more people, instead of immediately turning your heart off toward them.

LET GOD LEAD

When I moved out of my hometown, everything changed for me. I started a new job in a new city and was surrounded by new people. I attended a large church with multiple campuses, thousands of people, and hundreds of good men. How could I ever meet them all? Even if I did, how could I get to know each of them on a deep level? Obviously, I couldn't.

I was overwhelmed with the number of options I had. So I prayed. I asked God to put me in the right social circles where I would meet the people He wanted me to meet.

That prayer served a dual purpose.

First, I needed friends. It had taken me eighteen years to build relationships in my hometown, and it was going to take time to build some in this new city.

Second, I wanted to meet quality men who had the potential to be more than just a friend. So I made my prayer even more specific. I created a handwritten list of men who liked me or had asked me on a date. Alongside that, I wrote down names of men I didn't know but was interested in learning more about.

I prayed over that list, asking God to help me get to know them better so I could either cross them off or develop a deeper friendship with them. I ended up in their social circles at parties or other events where I was able to determine if there was something more than friendship between us.

THE SCARY THING ABOUT LETTING GOD CHOOSE FOR US IS THAT WE'RE AFRAID HE'LL GIVE US THE MAN WITH THE SHEPHERD'S STAFF IN HIS HAND RATHER THAN THE MAN WITH THE IMPRESSIVE CROWN ON HIS HEAD.

I put Sean on that list, but immediately crossed him off because I was already good friends with him and knew there was no future with him. Silly me.

The scary thing about letting God choose for us is that we're afraid He'll give us the man with the shepherd's staff in his hand rather than the man with the impressive crown on his head.

And even though you're so much more mature than your fifteen-year-old self, you're still worried God will choose someone ugly. Who wants that? So you subconsciously remain in control even though you tell God He's in control.

We're in this figurative fight with the Holy Spirit because we're afraid of who He's going to choose for us. If we're honest with ourselves, can we admit that we simply don't trust Him to choose well?

God had chosen Sean for me. But if I hadn't been intentional in my prayer life, and allowed the Holy Spirit to speak to my heart, I wouldn't have been able to detect the king within him.

To give the reigns over to God, get rid of the kingly image that exists in your mind. Then ask God to replace it with His image of what He wants for you. Doing this will help you recognize when a king is pursuing you, even if he is currently tending sheep.

David was a servant, an unknown. But he was a man after God's heart, righteous, humble, and pure. If God thought he was worthy of being king, don't you think He can find someone good enough for you?

Accept that God chooses differently than you. Otherwise, it's too easy to accept or reject someone based only on his appearance and accolades.

SETTLE FOR THE SHEPHERD BOY

My friend Bethany decided to marry a man who was a few years younger than she was. He was living at home and still trying to figure out his career. Shortly into their dating relationship, they found out he had cancer. This forced them to make decisions about their commitment and love for each other.

Bethany took care of him as he went through chemo and supported him as he pursued different career options. He was a faithful man of God, fighting for his life. But she wondered whether she was ready to commit to "till death do us part" if his cancer took a turn for the worse.

After giving it some thought and prayer, she felt confident enough in her feelings for him to make that commitment.

Bethany chose to love a shepherd on his way to becoming a king, even without any guarantee that he would get there. What she didn't know is that God would speak to him about starting a business and beginning a career as a successful entrepreneur.

Though he's still battling cancer, he and Bethany are married and deeply in love. They recently welcomed their first baby into their lives.

Bethany was able to see the king within and trust that this man was the right one for her, even if he wasn't quite as established as she'd hoped.

Many women are looking for a king who has already fulfilled his potential because it's too risky to marry a shepherd who hasn't. It can be difficult to see the anointing on someone if what's in front of us doesn't seem very kingly. Yet it's vital to see that potential. Because it's easier to fall in love when we believe a man is called to something more.

Don't ignore a guy simply because he hasn't reached his potential yet. On the other hand, don't fall in love with the potential of a man if you don't love who he is right now.

As a woman ages, the potential of a man becomes more of a deciding factor in whether she gives him her time and attention. Typically, a woman in her thirties isn't interested in a man who is still trying to figure out his career while working unimpressive jobs, doesn't own a home, is in debt, and drives a broken-down car.

I get that it's much more appealing to marry "David" while he's the king. You get to live in the palace, you don't have to worry about King Saul murdering your man, and you can enjoy the luxurious life David spent years fighting for. In modern-day terms, a king is successful, established, goal-oriented, and, for the most part, has things figured out.

But it took David about fifteen years before he fulfilled his anointing as king over all Israel. You don't have that kind of time to wait for a shepherd to turn into a king. But if you accept and love the man God has anointed for you, he can grow into his kingly capacity with you by his side.

GOD'S STANDARDS VS. SOCIETY'S STANDARDS

Too often we give our heart, affection, and attention to kings devoid of shepherdly qualities because we filter our attractions through societal standards first, God's standards second.

Societal standards are the subconscious criteria we have ingrained inside of us. When a person doesn't live up to the image we've created regarding looks, wealth, job, charisma, social status, and so on, we may not even realize that these things are leading our decision-making process.

The voice of the media, magazines, celebrities, and movies has become louder than the voice of God. We say yes or no to someone based on these qualifications, and then blame God because He hasn't brought us a spouse yet.

Did God tell you not to even consider a man who already has children? Or is that your own standard? Did God tell you not to date any man who's in debt? Or is that the standard your pastor gave you? Did God tell you not to settle for a man who doesn't come from a great family? Or is that your mom's standard?

WE SAY YES OR NO TO SOMEONE BASED ON THESE QUALIFICATIONS, AND THEN BLAME GOD BECAUSE HE HASN'T BROUGHT US A SPOUSE YET.

You aren't all-knowing, like God. Even if you have a good idea of what you need in a spouse, you don't know exactly what that is. Only He does.

Taylor, a friend of mine, was waiting for a savvy businessman to come into her life and sweep her off her feet. But the men she came in contact with didn't meet the character standards she had in mind.

When Taylor met her future husband, he wasn't a savvy businessman. But he was dependable, trustworthy, and true to his word. A man of character who would be an amazing husband and father. Taylor's perspective changed as she realized the long-lasting importance of marrying a man who would build a home filled with peace, grace, and love.

She could've walked away from this guy because he didn't have the businessman qualities she wanted. Instead, she allowed herself to fall in love with a man who deserved her affection. She chose God's standards over society's. And she has never regretted her decision to marry him.

My friend Tiffany has a similar story, but her qualifications were more specific. She was absolutely certain she didn't want to marry a man who had been divorced or had children from a previous relationship. Oh, and he couldn't have any tattoos. She came up with these qualifiers as a result of being influenced by what our culture told her would bring baggage into her marriage.

When Tiffany fell in love with a divorced father with tattoos, she didn't immediately determine that he wasn't an option for her. Instead, she got to know him and found that he was a man of integrity who had an amazing relationship with Jesus. His godly characteristics completely overshadowed the fact that he was a divorced father with tattoos, and she became deeply attracted to him. Her original list of nonnegotiables no longer mattered because she realized they weren't given to her by God.

Tiffany would say that her husband is better than her dream man! And God rewarded her for prioritizing His standards over her own. Now she's happily married with a beautiful daughter and is so thankful she gave her husband a chance.

Both Tiffany and Taylor knew God's standards mattered most. But many women have a filtering process that is backward while on the search for the man of their dreams. They want shepherds who meet all of God's standards, in addition to everything on their kingly list. They want it all.

You may be wondering, *What's wrong with that?* Well, problems arise when we give priority to society's standards, not God's.

When I was single, I was blind to that truth. I couldn't figure out why I rarely liked any guy as more than a friend. The truth was, I was waiting for the perfect person to come along.

I was attracted to men who were driven and highly ambitious. I wanted a man who was successful in his career and had all the connections I felt I needed to fulfill my dreams. I wanted him to have a nice car and own a home or at least be saving for one. I wanted him to be financially stable. He didn't have to be rich, just smart and secure. And he needed to be physically fit and attractive.

Sean didn't meet every demand on my list. And that bothered me.

Yet I didn't have all my ducks in a row either. I had recently stopped pursuing a career in ministry and was reevaluating my work life. I felt as if I was in the process of a midlife career change and wasn't sure how to blend my passion for ministry with this new season of life I was entering. At the age of twenty-six, I decided to get my bachelor's degree at the University of Washington while interning at a few different companies.

My day-to-day life had shifted from constant sameness to constant change, which felt unsettling and chaotic. I wanted a partner who had everything figured out so we could enjoy some stability together. Instead, Sean and I met when we were both going through life changes.

I almost walked away from Sean because of my filtering process.

Most Christian women tell themselves their godly standards take priority. But sometimes they have a ridiculous list of qualifications, often influenced by society. And they think it's better to remain single than to marry someone who doesn't have everything on that list.

Instead of having a realistic, Holy Spirit–led list, they hold on to *their* lists because they don't want to settle for anything "less." As a result, too many shepherds are overlooked because they don't have enough kingly qualities to cause these women to notice them.

It's as if they logically know there is no perfect man who has it all, yet they've been waiting for him for years and still aren't married. They aren't ready to relinquish their standards …. until their desire for marriage and family becomes greater than their desire for the ideal man.

If you choose to be open to the leading of the Holy Spirit, you could actually fall in love with someone who isn't exactly the man of your dreams. Someone who doesn't have it all together. Someone who isn't rich. Maybe someone who is never going to be wildly successful. He might not even have a job that will allow you to stay at home with your babies.

THEY AREN'T READY TO RELINQUISH THEIR STANDARDS …. UNTIL THEIR DESIRE FOR MARRIAGE AND FAMILY BECOMES GREATER THAN THEIR DESIRE FOR THE IDEAL MAN.

But isn't having love and commitment more of an abundant life than waiting for a picture-perfect future? Giving and receiving unconditional love, and working through life together, is worth it ... even if you have to put up with someone else's shortcomings and inadequacies.

Men usually become better after they've been married for a few years. If you find a man who is unselfish, knows how to live well with a woman, understands what women want in a relationship, and takes the trash out when asked, he's probably been married for a while. As a general rule of thumb, single men simply aren't as mature relationally as married men.

And believe it or not, you're not as relationally mature as you could be either. These characteristics are developed over time. Sean would say he is more emotionally healthy, is more considerate, has had more stable jobs, and has made more money as a married man than when he was single. And I have become kinder, more compassionate and affectionate, and more emotionally available.

In a healthy marriage, you both learn to love unconditionally, give generously, fight fairly, and compromise daily. You become more selfless and get better at loving the way Jesus loves. Men become more responsible about providing financial and relational security to the family.

When you get married, you choose to deal with your spouse's flaws and love him in spite of them. You join a man in his shepherd stage and then walk through the journey of life together.

REASSESS YOUR CHOOSING PROCESS

If you're beginning to realize that some of your preconceived standards don't really matter after all, it's time to question why they are what they are. Then you can determine whether your filtering process is accurate or backward.

The first step is to figure out what you're attracted to, and why you do or don't like someone.

Take a look at the inventory of men who meet God's standards for you. These are the ones you should give your attention to. Have you befriended them? Initiated conversations? Asked for their phone numbers?

If you are not drawn to these men, search your heart for an answer as to why. Ask yourself if there are any societal standards that you can compromise in. If you refuse to let them be deal breakers, your heart will be open to more people—the right kind of people—and your feelings of attraction will follow.

I had to actively seek the Holy Spirit to guide my attractions. I spent a lot of time praying, fasting, and waiting, which helped keep God at the center of my focus.

Sean and I fit God's standards for each other, and that helped us make our decision to get married. We saw that we each had a personal relationship with Jesus, we loved ministry, and we were people of character and integrity. When I began prioritizing God's standards, He turned my heart toward Sean.

We're still on our way to fulfilling our roles and responsibilities in this life. We challenge each other, encourage each other, and support each other. And we're doing that together.

CHAPTER 5

THE 90 PERCENTER

S ay you have a friend everyone seems to like. She's kind
and friendly, pretty and popular, with an outgoing
personality. You feel good when you're around her because
she's encouraging and makes you feel at ease. She listens
well, yet also has interesting things to talk about.

She's what I call a 90 percenter. Ninety percent of
the men she comes in contact with want to date her.
They think she's the perfect girl for them. Her beauty
overshadows whatever flaws she may have.

A man can be a 90 percenter too. He is attractive and
charismatic. He enjoys social settings. He's ambitious, a
man with purpose, who knows where he's going and how
to get what he wants. He's been saving for the perfect
engagement ring. And he'll definitely make beautiful
babies.

Men want to be his friend and women want to date
him. Most women won't pursue this kind of guy. But they
would happily respond if he pursued them.

Whenever one of my single friends tells me she has a
crush, I almost always know who it is. It's the guy who has
a steady job, loves Jesus, and is socially smooth. He's either
got a lot of money or a noble pursuit, such as mission

work, education, or ministry. He is intelligent and kind, and he comes from a great family.

I'm not describing the perfect man or woman. I'm describing one of the best options you have in your social sphere. Maybe no one you know is going to be wealthy, maybe no one is stylish. But there are still 90 percenters in your world.

There was a short season of my life when I had many pursuers. Men asked me out, befriended me, and worked hard to turn our friendship into something romantic. That was a fun place to be. However, it was also discouraging because I wasn't interested in hardly any of them. Nothing was inherently wrong with these guys. I just wasn't attracted to them. I quickly realized that some of them were only drawn to me because of the image I presented. They weren't actually interested in me as a person. They didn't even know the real me.

If you're always attracted to 90 percenters, consider the possibility that you may not know them very well on the inside. If you did, you might not even like them. You just love the idea of them. And you love how you see yourself when you're with them.

WHY GET STUCK ON THAT RAT WHEEL? IT'S A RIDICULOUS CYCLE THAT KEEPS PEOPLE FROM MAKING ANY PROGRESS IN THE DATING WORLD.

I'm reminded of a scene in the movie *Dumb and Dumber*, where Lloyd asks Mary what kind of chance he has of ending up with her. Her response is that he has about a one-in-a-million chance. Even though that answer is an obvious no, he still thinks he's got a shot.[1]

He's the kind of guy I want to put in front of a mirror and say, "Look! You don't have a chance with her! And here's why."

I understand that sounds cruel, but why couldn't Lloyd like someone who was quirky and crazy like him? Why did he have to go for the girl everyone else wanted?

Because he wanted the ideal woman, the one who fits society's standards of beautiful and acceptable—the 90 percenter. If he was more realistic with himself, he might have found a wonderful girl who fit him perfectly and was the best option *for him*.

Not everyone needs to be vying for the Marys of the world, hoping for the chance of a lifetime and waiting to be swept off their feet.

Why get stuck on that rat wheel? It's a ridiculous cycle that keeps people from making any progress in the dating world. It's time to wake up.

As Christians we're taught, "God has the best for you. So don't settle for His permissive will. Instead, wait for His perfect will. You're a child of God; therefore, you deserve the best."

But there's a problem with applying this mind-set to dating. *There is always someone better.* And what is the "best" anyway?

You can always find a more attractive man, someone more adventurous, someone sweeter and kinder than your last crush, a guy who's more romantic than the one

---

1   *Dumb and Dumber*, DVD, directed by Peter Farrelly (New York City, NY: New Line Cinema, 1995).

you're currently dating. There is always someone better, so in the back of your mind, you'll always be looking for the "best."

No one wants to settle for less than best. But labeling someone as the best devalues the worth of other human beings. Do you think God looks at your social sphere and labels some individuals as better than others? Of course not. We're the ones who do that.

We assume God qualifies one man as better than the other in the same way that we would say a Mercedes is better than a Ford.

Second Corinthians 10:12 (NIV) says, "We do not dare to classify or compare ourselves with some who commend themselves. When they measure themselves by themselves and compare themselves with themselves, they are not wise." When we compare men to one another, we become dissatisfied with the options of eligible guys out there.

And when you hear that quiet voice in your heart telling you that a certain nonnegotiable you have on your list doesn't actually matter, you ignore it, holding out hope for that 90 percenter. After all, you are God's princess, right? So you aim for the stars and go for guys who are "out of your league." That attractive athlete and wealthy businessman has to marry someone. Why not you?

You tell yourself you're waiting for Mr. Right, but you're only interested in Mr. Perfect. This way of thinking has kept many women single. God isn't a genie in a bottle, dispensing men who have all the qualities you desire. If you wait for it all, you may end up with nothing.

And you'd better hope your future husband isn't waiting for the perfect woman, or he may never find you.

YOU TELL YOURSELF YOU'RE WAITING FOR MR. RIGHT, BUT YOU'RE ONLY INTERESTED IN MR. PERFECT.

Why are some women only interested in the 90 percenters who seem to have it all? Usually it's because they aren't able to look objectively at themselves and acknowledge that they might have attributes that a 90 percenter wouldn't be attracted to. Or because they're so insecure that they think being with a 90 percenter will give them the confidence boost they need in life.

THE INABILITY TO BE OBJECTIVE

The qualities we want in others are the ones we believe we have in ourselves, or wish we had. They are the qualities we believe we deserve. But you may not be what your perfect man is looking for. The gorgeous, popular, outgoing, wealthy guy may be your type, but you might not be his type.

FOCUSING ON WHAT MAKES YOU UNIQUE AND SPECIAL WILL HELP YOU BE HONEST IN YOUR ASSESSMENT OF WHO YOU'LL BEST FIT WITH.

Has a friend ever set you up with a really dorky guy? Did that make you wonder what your friend must think about you? Does she see you as some plain Jane who couldn't possibly get a more popular guy? If she thought you had a chance with that 90 percenter you've been fantasizing about, she'd tell him about you. There must be a reason she hasn't.

It's possible that the most popular guy in your social sphere views you as a plain, noncharismatic girl, especially in comparison to others.

And your girlfriends are usually able to see your beauty and greatness much more easily than men. Especially men you don't even know. So even if your bestie tells you you're hot, that doesn't mean your crush has the same taste she does.

Have a realistic view of yourself. Know your strengths. Focusing on what makes you unique and special will help you be honest in your assessment of who you'll best fit with.

LACKING IN CONFIDENCE

We all feel a bit more confident if we have a strong, good-looking, successful man on our arm, shouting our praises from the rooftop. Our confidence surges when a prestigious man gives us attention. But our confidence shouldn't depend on that.

And even if you were to snag him, he couldn't solve your insecurity issues. Problems would surface in your marriage.

If your confidence is dependent on other people, things, or circumstances, it will always be shaky. You'll end up dating guys other people are impressed by just to feel good about yourself. Or you'll create a new identity merely to catch a guy's attention. You'll become a chameleon, fitting into his mold in order to get what you want. You'll come up with new likes, dislikes, and passions. And you may not even realize you're doing it!

If the 90 percenter you're attracted to is a dog person, even if you've always loved cats, you become a dog person. He loves the outdoors, but you're a homebody. Hiking suddenly becomes your favorite pastime. He's a city boy; you're a farm girl. You develop a passion for big-city life.

Of course, we all make compromises to accommodate the guys we like. It's okay to adjust certain personality traits that might be hindering you from making friends or getting asked out.

But if you're going to increase the number of romantic options you have, it has to start with you. Becoming more confident in who you are enables you to consider guys who might not be as cool or successful as others.

Besides, confident people can be friends with the unpopular; insecure people cannot.

TIME TO MOVE ON

Too many women choose a boyfriend the way they'd hire a candidate for a job. They review his résumé, look at his past experiences, and see if he's qualified for the work at hand. They quickly assess his career, family, possessions, goals, friends, and overall potential.

They wonder what his previous girlfriends were like and how many girls he's dated. How many other "job interviews" has he gone on? Was their "job opening" on the top of his list, or are they his second or third choice because his application was turned down at other places?

But a woman can't find the right person just by checking off boxes. A guy's résumé might look perfect in the beginning. But résumés only showcase the applicant's highlights. And some of those highlights are exaggerated.

If you're choosing men based on their "résumés" rather than whether you care about them, you may be more interested in a secure relationship than being with a man you love.

In order to move on from choosing a man based on his résumé, you'll need to narrow down your list of requirements.

Start "interviewing" men who aren't 90 percenters. And accepting guys with flaws. You might be surprised at who you could actually fall in love with.

When you're happy with the real you, you'll find the right person. And the right person will be attracted to you.

CHAPTER 6

GIVE SOMEONE A SHOT WHO'S NOT RICH AND HOT

One afternoon, I was sitting with friends at a restaurant, discussing one of the most important things in life: relationships. We were deep in conversation when one of the girls mentioned an epiphany she'd recently had.

After nearly three decades of having little to no interest in most men, she realized she was deciding whether she liked someone based on how attractive and financially secure he was. She didn't realize she was filtering out prospective men based on these qualifications. But a pattern had developed that proved this to be true.

Like her, many people are unaware how important these standards are to them. They choose to pursue or respond to men based on one or both.

MONEY MATTERS

For women, the idea of being taken care of financially is appealing. We've all had jobs we've hated, and it takes time and effort to excel at work you actually enjoy. The thought of leaving the rat race behind and staying home to raise children causes many single women to look for a man who makes enough money to support a family.

Many men experience the same career frustrations as women. It's no fun going to work every day and doing a job you're not passionate about. However, men are expected to be the breadwinners, so they're more likely to accept the difficulties and frustrations that come along with fulfilling that role.

This dynamic is changing, and more women make just as much as, if not more than, their husbands. But in general, women are more eager to be taken care of financially and men are usually okay with fulfilling that expectation.

A lot of women say they don't care how much money a guy makes. But others hold out hope for a man who is independently wealthy. Some want a husband who has a successful business with a flexible schedule so they can have his time, his money, and the luxury of staying at home with their children. What woman wants a man who can't afford to put food on the table?

Let's look at four types of women and how they approach relationships in regards to money.

The Gold Digger

You have expensive taste. You are an excellent shopper, and the American economy flourishes thanks to your contributions. To you, a man's financial status is a huge part of whether you choose to date him. You don't have any interest in learning how to budget. Or changing your spending habits.

Or maybe you came from a wealthy family and love the feel of cashmere next to your skin. In your twenties, when you got out on your own, you went into debt trying to keep up with your familiar, comfortable lifestyle. It would be great to find a man who loves you enough to pay off your debt and give you a clean slate.

Either way, you're never attracted to someone who isn't on the fast track to success.

Could be that's why you're still single.

If your foundation for marriage is based on love rather than money, consider dating a man who isn't financially established yet. If you don't, you might not recognize the person God has for you.

THE WELL-MEANING WOMAN

Wealth may not be a deal breaker for you, but you are hopeful that your future husband will have *some* money. After all, you're not really interested in men with mediocre jobs that don't pay much.

On first dates, you ask the man what he wants to do with his life. What are his dreams and goals? If he says he's a cashier, you're not interested in a second date. His unimpressive job has caused you to view him as an unimpressive human being.

HIS UNIMPRESSIVE JOB HAS CAUSED YOU TO VIEW HIM AS AN UNIMPRESSIVE HUMAN BEING.

You want a man who is going somewhere, has ambition, and can provide a secure financial future for his family. You tell yourself the main reason you don't like this guy is that he doesn't have direction. But you don't really know him. You've just assumed that he lacks vision because he doesn't have an amazing job.

THE SELF-MADE WOMAN

You've worked hard to put yourself through school and climb the corporate ladder, and now you're reaping the rewards.

You want a man who is just as successful as you, if not more so. You couldn't respect a man who has eaten from a golden spoon his entire life when you had to dig for the gold, fashion the spoon, and then feed yourself with it. You want a man with the same ability, willpower, and drive you have.

But do you really want to marry someone who is exactly like you? Life's more fun when you partner up with someone who has different personality traits, strengths, and weaknesses. You'll complement each other, not merely be male and female versions of each other.

Families in which both parents have demanding jobs and a similar drive for success have many positives. They can afford fun vacations and nice things, for example. But there are also negatives. They have to pay for day care or a full-time nanny. They have limited time and energy to spend with their children. The pressure of their jobs can be very stressful. They may have competing ambitions, which can cause division in their relationship. And they might receive more respect and admiration from work than at home, which can cause resentment.

Marrying someone who's not as successful as you are isn't such a bad thing. What you've considered unattractive could be exactly what you need.

THE IN-LOVE-WITH-LOVE WOMAN

To you, love makes the world go 'round. You love the idea of building a life based on love. Finances and other practical necessities will follow.

Before my sister married her husband, he told her she'd better be okay living on a tight budget because he planned to work on the family farm, and farmers don't make a lot of money. She wanted to stay at home with the kids, so she agreed. They're happily married today, with six children, living on a farmer's income.

Money doesn't have to make or break a marriage. Love truly is what holds it together.

If you agree to marry a guy without money, don't change your mind five years into the marriage. Know yourself and what you can handle.

WHY YOU CHOOSE WHAT YOU CHOOSE

Eventually, the above types of women start shaving off "must-haves" from their lists. And the amount of money a man makes is usually one of the first things to go.

Why wait to realize it's more important for you to start a family with a man you love than it is for you to have a wealthy Prince Charming?

Start by putting your desire for financial security toward the bottom of the list so you can recognize the right man when he comes along, even if he's not well-off.

And in the process, ask yourself why money is so important to you.

Would you think less of yourself if you couldn't snag a man who was able to take care of you financially? Perhaps your family wouldn't approve. Is it because you'd be embarrassed if he didn't make a lot of money? Maybe you're tired of being independent and want to be taken care of. Or maybe it's as simple as craving financial stability for your family.

Whatever your reason, consider this. A successful career is not a guarantee of financial success for a lifetime. Anyone can be laid off or lose his ability to continue working. What if your husband decides to change his career path ten years into your marriage? Will you still love him?

Financial success at the beginning of a relationship is never a guarantee that you'll have money for the rest of your life. So if you're waiting for a wealthy someone, you may be single for a long time. Or you might get to the point where money isn't all that important to you.

After all, having wealth doesn't mean that everything in life is going to be great.

When I was twenty-five, I worked as a nanny for a woman who lived in an affluent neighborhood. Through that job, I got to know several of the other moms in the area, which gave me insight into the lives of wealthy women and their families.

One lady I met was very down-to-earth. She didn't drive a flashy car, and her kids had practical, inexpensive things rather than everything top-of-the-line.

Many of the other moms worked full time at demanding jobs and had nannies. But this gal was a stay-at-home mom who only hired an occasional babysitter.

What made this woman different was that she used to be poor. She was previously married to an alcoholic man who couldn't take care of his family. She vividly remembers feeding her daughter and husband the little food they had, opting to go without because there wasn't enough for her.

BUT IF YOUR DESIRE FOR WEALTH IS SO POTENT THAT YOU NEVER SEEM TO NOTICE THE CHARACTER QUALITY OF THE MEN YOU'RE SURROUNDED BY, IT'S HIGH TIME YOU ADJUSTED YOUR EXPECTATIONS AND PRIORITIZED LOVE.

After divorcing her alcoholic husband, she fell in love with a wealthy man who had an Ivy League education. She and her rich husband went on nice vacations, but they hardly got to spend any time together because it took him several days to wind down. And even during their trips, he didn't stop working. So she and the kids did fun activities together without him.

This made her angry. But she realized she couldn't change him. Besides, she loved him.

This woman knew what it was like to be poor and to be rich. She'd experienced the fear and frustrations that come with a lack of finances, and the peace of mind and security that money brings. But both lifestyles had their downfalls.

Now, there is nothing inherently wrong with money. But if your desire for wealth is so potent that you never seem to notice the character quality of the men you're surrounded by, it's high time you adjusted your expectations and prioritized love.

ACTIONS SPEAK LOUDER THAN WORDS

If you don't consider yourself to be the type of person who judges people based on money, take a look at your actions. Actions often communicate things we aren't willing to admit to ourselves.

Have you ever moved beyond friendship with someone who wasn't financially secure? Do you fantasize about snagging a rich boyfriend?

Growing up, I told myself I didn't care about money, but based on my actions, that wasn't really true.

When I met Sean, he was working for his parents as a business development manager and also had a part-time job as a salesman at a clothing store. He acknowledged that he wasn't making enough money, so I wondered why he didn't get a job in his career path that paid more. I assumed he was apathetic, and I didn't want to date someone like that.

I later found out that the reason he had those two jobs was that he needed the flexibility they provided. Working from home for his parents and at odd hours for the clothing store allowed him to be involved in his church's leadership. And he believed God had called him to ministry.

He viewed himself as a hard worker obeying the call of God, while I viewed him as unmotivated and carefree when it came to money.

My judgment of him was wrong. If I had discovered his dreams earlier, I may have developed feelings for him sooner.

If a man with an unimpressive job likes you, give him a chance. Take the time to get to know him. Find out his goals and ambitions. Do a little digging before you delete him from your list.

Many men have great plans for accumulating wealth but are quiet about them. They don't want to impress a girl who just wants a boyfriend with money so she can get expensive gifts for her birthday.

RESPECT WHOMEVER YOU CHOOSE

When Sean and I began dating, he was thousands of dollars in debt. I didn't have any debt. I wasn't rich, but I was frugal.

After handling my finances wisely, did I deserve to be connected to someone who didn't? No.

But soon after we started dating, I took a part-time job and went back to school. Paying my apartment lease became difficult. I barely had enough money for food and gas. Sean, who had more money than I did at that point, drove me everywhere and paid for all of our dates, so I hardly spent any money.

I think that was God's sovereign plan, because it caused me to need Sean financially during that time, which led me to respect him far more than I would have otherwise.

Though I didn't realize it, what I needed was someone who was more relaxed than I was, who was better at enjoying life, less disciplined, more fun, less critical.

During the first year of our marriage, Sean got a different job, which brought in a great income. We managed to pay off all of his debt, including his car payment.

Later, he put me through school while I was working at internships that paid little to no money. I was able to stay home with our first daughter because his income supported all three of us.

I took a chance and trusted God with the results. And He rewarded me for that.

Similarly, my friend Sarah grew up poor and spent much of her adult life assisting her family financially. She made more than most men. But she wanted to find a husband who made more money than she did.

When she began dating her future husband, she realized this desire was unrealistic and rooted in fear.

My friend Bethany, in her early thirties, had been working in her career for years. She'd lived on her own for a decade and owned her own home. She expected to marry a man who had a lifestyle comparable to hers. But she became attracted to a man five years younger than she was and who still lived with his parents.

My friends and I were hard-working, intelligent, successful, independent women who thought we deserved established men who had it all. But we made exceptions to our expectations because we chose to accept the men

PART THREE

LET'S GO FISHING!

Fishermen know how to catch fish. Basically, they find a spot where the fish hang out, put the right bait on the hook, and cast their line into the water. Then they wait.

You know how to catch a man, right? You go to where they hang out. You put the right bait on the hook and you cast your line. And wait. Eventually, the right bait brings you the right mate. But if you've been sitting on the same dock day in and day out, casting your line with no success, you're probably starting to wonder what you're doing wrong.

To be fair, there are some slimy, nasty fish out there that seem to have polluted the whole lake. But there are still some good-quality fish left. They're just not easy to catch.

This section offers practical steps to help you be the best you can be so you can lure in the good fish. If you follow the steps outlined in this section, and are open to the type of men who respond to your bait, I believe you'll find a mate that's right for you.

CHAPTER 7

BAIT #1: BE INTERESTED

When I was single, I noticed how girls interacted with guys at parties. I could always tell which women had no problem befriending men. They'd ask questions, listen, laugh—it seemed like they genuinely enjoyed getting to know someone new. I also noticed the girls who congregated with each other and seemed uncomfortable or uninterested in the single men there.

I wondered why they preferred to talk with one another when there were available men in the room. I realize that it's easier, and sometimes more fun, to catch up with your girlfriends at a party than it is to meet single guys. It's often exhausting or boring to make small talk with strangers.

But genuine interest in another person will cause him or her to feel comfortable. When I showed I was curious about a particular guy, even if I wasn't romantically attracted to him, I didn't come across as "too cool."

Good conversations with the opposite sex don't have to be based solely on attraction. So whether or not you like a particular guy, show interest in him simply because he is a human being.

SO WHETHER OR NOT YOU LIKE A PARTICULAR GUY, SHOW INTEREST IN HIM SIMPLY BECAUSE HE IS A HUMAN BEING.

MAKE A FRIEND

Single people are often bombarded with questions about who they're dating. Family members pressure them about settling down. People tell them they're going on too many dates, or not enough. Eventually, the pursuit of marriage becomes all-consuming.

Marriage is wonderful. It brings you a sense of fulfillment and joy, and it's a noble, godly aspiration. But the pressure to get married can stress people out, causing them to cry themselves to sleep at night, making them feel like they're disappointing their parents, and getting them to think they're not good enough.

To avoid this, shift your focus from marriage to friendship, viewing men as friends first, rather than potential boyfriends. This way, you can get to know a guy without the pressure of determining if he qualifies as a lifelong partner. You'll also be less judgmental because you won't be going through a mental checklist of whether or not he's good enough for you. And you'll probably find a spouse much easier if you're not thinking about marriage all the time.

Once a guy is your friend, you'll get to know who he is on the inside—his integrity, kindness, humor—and he'll probably become more attractive to you. Then you can begin the potential dating process. And as your number of male friends grows, you'll have more chances at eventually meeting your husband.

When you see a guy you want to get to know, take steps to get into his world. Initiate conversation with him, become friends with his friends, invite him to a party you're going to, or simply say hi to him when you see him. If none of those strategies works, pray for opportunities to be around him.

If you don't actively pursue friendship with the opposite sex, guys will view you as either uninterested or stuck up. Men feel much more comfortable chasing a girl who can confidently engage in interesting conversation than one who comes across as bitter or seems to think she's better than every man out there.

But don't force a friendship to happen. You don't need to incessantly tag along uninvited, or always ask him what he's doing and whether you can join. If there's no reciprocation in a friendship with you, don't waste your time. Move on.

FRIENDSHIP BLOCKERS

I grew up in a house with five kids: an older sister and three younger brothers. I wasn't intimidated by men because I was familiar with their behaviors. So it was easy for me to have guy friends.

But you may find it difficult to communicate with guys because you don't understand them. Do you often feel awkward around men? When you see other girls having easy conversations with guys, do you envy that? Let's explore some reasons this happens.

FRIENDSHIP BLOCKER #1: FAMILY HISTORY

Did you have a good relationship with your dad when you were growing up? Was he around often or rarely? Were your relationships with your brothers or other male family members healthy? If the men you knew growing up hurt you, cheated on you, or abused you, you may find it hard to make male friends as an adult. And you might not believe that you will find a good man someday.

It's hard to trust men when that trust has been broken.

If you haven't known a man who unconditionally loved you, respected you, treasured you, and was faithful and loyal to you, let God heal those wounds before you try to build genuine friendships with men.

The first step might be to see a counselor to discuss your wounds and how they're affecting your current relationships. This can be a painful process, but it's necessary in order to understand why you act the way you do, especially around certain men. Also, spending consistent time with the Holy Spirit will help you more deeply experience God's love for you. Doing this will give you greater discernment in recognizing the type of man you can trust.

It may still feel like a risk to let a man in, but as your past hurts begin to heal, you'll be more willing to take that chance with men who exhibit the fruits of the Spirit: love, joy, peace, patience, kindness, goodness, faithfulness, gentleness, and self-control (Galatians 5:22–23). As you become friends with godly men, you'll have more faith in the prospect of finding that amazing partner in life.

FRIENDSHIP BLOCKER #2: A CERTAIN TYPE

Maybe you're only good at befriending men who are chauvinistic, judgmental, and cruel. Or you seem to attract the player and commitment-phobe types. These guys are the ones you're most comfortable around and familiar with. Whether your experience with them is based on your growing-up years or your pre-Christian days, you've only dated and been friends with this kind of guy.

Of course, that's not the kind of man you want to date and marry. But when a man comes along who has a healthy soul, who loves Jesus, is emotionally stable, is kind, and respects women, you clam up and don't know how to be yourself.

It's like a poor person going to a rich person's party. You aren't sure how to converse with people who have it all. You don't feel like you have anything in common. You're stressed about which fork to use and when. You feel incredibly awkward because you've never been around rich people. So you became an observer at that party.

In order to get more comfortable with the type of man you want to date, remind yourself that you're a righteous, godly woman. You *are* good enough. Even if a relationship doesn't work out, that doesn't mean you aren't worthy.

If you find yourself experiencing feelings of condemnation for your past wrongs, know that God has forgiven you if you've sought His forgiveness. You are no longer a good match for the type of men you used to date.

Accept your new self and confidently pursue friendships with the godly men you admire.

FRIENDSHIP BLOCKER #3: "OFF THE MARKET" MEN

Maybe you only feel comfortable around guys who are already taken. When you hang out with your girlfriend and her husband, you can behave like your normal, charming self because you know he's not available. You aren't concerned with what he's thinking about you. You aren't trying to impress him, nor are you worried that he's judging you. You don't care how cute you look in front of him. You can be yourself without the fear of not being accepted by him.

When I was single, I found it easier to be my usual friendly self with guys who weren't Christians because I knew I would never marry them. I went on a few dates with guys who didn't share my faith. I enjoyed my time with them and built friendships with them. I even brought some of my guy friends to church with me.

But whenever I became interested in a Christian guy, there was an immediate sense of anxiety, fear, and pressure. I didn't want to ruin a potential friendship, but if the relationship was going well, there was always an underlying fear of commitment. As much as I wanted to fall in love, I was afraid to.

If you find it easy to be normal only around "off the market" men because you don't feel any pressure to commit, stop thinking about what he's thinking. When you're wondering how the other person views you, you can't show genuine interest because you're consumed with yourself. It's mentally exhausting wondering if you're going to be accepted by a man you don't even know very well.

If you think of him as a friend who has already approved of you, you won't find yourself obsessing over his thoughts about you. Then you can more naturally approach a friendship with him.

BACK TO THE BASICS

A man won't know who you are after just a few conversations. So if you like a guy, take the initiative. Ask for his phone number, or invite him out for coffee. Going after a friendship with a man is not the same thing as pursuing him romantically.

Initiate once or twice, and if you gain a friend, great! If he doesn't return the favor, let it go and move on.

As you practice showing interest in the opposite sex, more men will like you and ask you out. So be bold and confident. We could all use more friends.

CHAPTER 8

BAIT #2: BE ATTRACTIVE

To gain the interest of the kind of man you want to date, make yourself attractive. Develop within yourself the qualities you desire in your future spouse. Do you want your man to be fashionable? Stay current with the trends. Do you want him to be in shape? Then hit the gym and have an active lifestyle.

Your looks might get you a date, but it's who you are on the inside that will keep a fish on the line until the hook is set. You don't need to have the perfect body or the prettiest face. The type of guys you want to notice you aren't looking for a supermodel.

Who you are on the inside will either accentuate or detract from your outer beauty. And who you are on the inside will likely attract someone similar to you on the inside.

If you're judgmental and demeaning, you'll draw in a man who has low self-esteem, lacks confidence, and is sometimes mean. If you're a strong, healthy woman who is confident, loving, kind, and gentle, you'll attract a man who is supportive and selfless. Women usually attract men who are on the same mental, emotional, and spiritual level.

WOMEN USUALLY ATTRACT MEN WHO ARE ON THE SAME MENTAL, EMOTIONAL, AND SPIRITUAL LEVEL.

BEYOND LOOKS

You can't fake integrity or character. Eventually, the real you will shine through.

Typically, men try to fake a beautiful inside more than women do. A guy will brag about the monthly donation he sent to a child in Africa. Or how much he prays or reads the Bible if the girl he likes is into church. But if a woman is intuitive and discerning, she'll know the truth.

Ironically, women tend to use external beauty to catch a man's attention. They get fake boobs, fake tans, fake nails, fake hair, a push-up bra, heavy makeup, Spanx, lash extensions, hair extensions, etc.

We may not all go to that extent, but we all crave beauty. And there's nothing wrong with wanting to be beautiful. But to attract a person who cares about inner beauty, you have to care about that too.

To help you make yourself attractive on the inside, I've compiled a list of seven traits that can be developed within.

LOVE FOR JESUS

Men who love Jesus are interested in women who love Jesus. However, Christian women sometimes get weary in waiting for a godly man to pursue them. So they make compromises. They date men who aren't actively pursuing a relationship with Jesus, who aren't able to be spiritual leaders in the home, and who don't share their definition of Christianity.

As they date ungodly men, these women make compromises in their own character, which makes them unattractive to the kind of godly men they originally held out hope for. A godly man is going to look for a woman who exhibits godly characteristics.

Think of a pyramid. The base, the widest point, represents all the eligible men in the world. Women who choose from the base of the pyramid have the most options because they have few standards or restrictions as to the type of men they're willing to marry.

But if you have standards for your spouse, you limit your options. If some of your standards are godliness and a genuine relationship with Jesus, you're choosing from the top of the pyramid.

The same goes for women who are only interested in men of the same ethnicity or cultural background, or men who have an Ivy league education, or men with a certain type of job. That's why it's important to prayerfully determine what standards are nonnegotiables.

Stay true to who you are and continue to strengthen your relationship with Jesus. This not only benefits you in your walk with God, it also maintains your attractiveness to those who share your beliefs.

CONFIDENCE

People with confidence are attractive. They know they have flaws, but they have learned to accept themselves and value themselves. They showcase their strengths instead of their weaknesses. They aren't mean or cruel. They believe that they'll be successful in life. They draw others to themselves without even trying.

Being around these people makes you feel confident as well. You never have to walk on eggshells around them because they are emotionally stable. They can handle an insult and deal with rude comments. They don't fall apart if their feelings get hurt.

That doesn't mean they're invincible and don't have emotions. But they know how to work through difficult seasons in life and can ask for help when needed.

THE KEY TO SELF-CONFIDENCE IS TO UNDERSTAND THAT YOU ARE LOVED AND ACCEPTED BY GOD FIRST, AND THEN TO SURROUND YOURSELF WITH PEOPLE WHO PROVIDE YOU WITH LOVE AND ACCEPTANCE.

On the other hand, insecure people depend on another person's approval in order to feel good about themselves. They're convinced others don't like them and are afraid of what others are thinking about them. It's hard for them to believe in themselves or expect good things to happen to them.

Confidence doesn't mean you think you're better than other people. Those who have inflated egos are imprisoned by constant comparison to others. Don't let yourself be drawn to the type of person who appears confident but only at the expense of someone else.

The key to self-confidence is to understand that you are loved and accepted by God first, and then to surround yourself with people who provide you with love and acceptance.

Confident people see the greatness inside everyone. Grow in your confidence and you'll grow in your friendships and your romantic prospects.

AMBITION AND GOALS

Women want their men to know where they're going in life. They want a man to know what he wants and how to get it.

However, our American culture makes us believe that fantasy can become reality. We can win the lottery; we can become millionaires by being on a reality show; we can catapult our careers by winning a televised competition. And when the truth hits us, we realize it's way more difficult to achieve success than we thought.

We eventually come to the realization that we can't live in poverty for the next ten years while working toward our dreams. So we get a job. Any ol' job.

Proverbs 29:18 (KJV) says, "Where there is no vision, the people perish." But we often confuse vision with accomplishment. If a man doesn't have a lot of accomplishments to brag about, that doesn't mean he doesn't have a vision from God.

IF A MAN DOESN'T HAVE A LOT OF ACCOMPLISHMENTS TO BRAG ABOUT, THAT DOESN'T MEAN HE DOESN'T HAVE A VISION FROM GOD.

Men pursue their vision at different paces. Yet many women want men who have already accomplished many things. But if a woman can't find a man who is further along in his accomplishments than she is, she may have to make compromises. She'll either need to accept a man who hasn't achieved as much as she has, or marry a man who's a lot older than she is.

Single women should have the same expectations for themselves regarding vision as they do for men. If you want it all, chances are he wants it all too. So what are you bringing to the table?

IF YOU WANT IT ALL, CHANCES ARE HE WANTS IT ALL TOO.

God has a plan for every individual in this world. Seek and follow His plan for you. If you don't have any other vision for your life besides getting married, connect with the Holy Spirit. He'll help you understand what His dreams are for you in your current season of life. This will bring you joy and will also result in you being more attractive to men with vision.

CHARMING PERSONALITY

Genuinely charming people are interested in learning about others, eager to please, and nonjudgmental. I think of politicians and pastors, who are typically talkative, friendly, and diplomatic. They know how to make people feel important and valued.

They have their own interests, so they don't have to gossip to have interesting conversations. They don't try to be intimidating, nor are they intimidated by others. They are funny, fun, and confident.

Unfortunately for all the single ladies, guys like this get picked off the market first. But as much as you might blame your singleness on the lack of quality men in your life, you can't control your surroundings. You can only control you. So …

How charming are you? Are you bold enough to talk to the new cute guy in your world? What about you is attractive and compelling?

To be charming means "to delight or fascinate, to be alluring or pleasing."[2] There's no harm in flirting a little with someone you're interested in so that he knows you like him.

If you aren't sure how to do this, get around people who have pursuers and mimic them. I'm not advocating being fake, but take an honest inventory of your charming traits, make adjustments where needed, and then step out of your comfort zone.

---

2   "Charming" definition, *The Free Dictionary*, http://www.thefreedictionary.com/charming.

KINDNESS

This trait is undervalued in our society. It's easily overshadowed by other more popular factors: a good job, humor, security, status, etc. Only if a man meets a plethora of other qualifications first is his kindness considered.

Don't forget to prioritize kindness in your search for a lifelong partner. That trait will last a lot longer than his six-pack abs.

My husband is the king of kindness. He believes that all people should be treated with respect, patience, and love.

I share this belief, but I make more exceptions than he does. For me, kindness is somewhat conditional. If someone is driving badly, or if I encounter poor customer service, I might lose my ability to be kind.

Unkind people are selfish. They get upset when circumstances don't revolve around them or when others inconvenience them.

I'll never be as kind as Sean because he is kinder by nature. But I'll always be working toward that goal. I'll follow his example to be a kinder, more loving, more selfless person.

If you're not uber sweet and know you never will be, that's okay. There are certain traits that others are better at. That just means you need to work on your patience and love toward others. Because when you're kind, people want to be around you.

ACCEPTANCE

To be accepted for who you are and loved in spite of your flaws is a treasure. When someone knows your mistakes and inadequacies and still accepts you, that person loves you unconditionally. This is the way Jesus loves.

People need to know they are loved and accepted even if they never change. When we practice this kind of love toward all sorts of people, we show compassion toward them.

I've experienced love like this from my husband and my family. It's not that my parents never corrected me or that my husband doesn't think I should change in some areas. They see those flaws, have pointed them out and discussed how I should change, yet they still love and accept me.

What an honor to feel loved in spite of your wrongs.

If you haven't been given this example from other people, receive Jesus' love and acceptance. Then follow His example and become accepting of others in the same way Jesus has accepted you. If you can demonstrate acceptance to everyone, people will be so drawn to you that you won't have enough time in your schedule to keep up with all the social requests.

Partner with those who can run alongside you on the journey, encouraging you, loving you, and helping you change. This will empower you to extend that same grace and acceptance toward others.

HUMOR AND HAPPINESS

Women love funny men. So most men do their best to entertain women.

But what does a good sense of humor really mean? For women, it usually means "Make me laugh." For men, it tends to mean "Laugh at my jokes (even if they're not very funny)."

It's a privilege to be with someone who can laugh through life. So make it a priority to find someone who encourages happiness and laughter. And strive to be that kind of person as well. Most men will be drawn to a fun, entertaining woman who laughs easily. It's difficult to be around a negative person who doesn't appear to enjoy life.

According to WebMD, laughter can "reduce the negative effects of feeling unhealthy, out of control, afraid, or helpless, which are problems for those with cancer or chronic diseases."[3] Humor therapy is used in hospitals to treat cancer and other diseases, and is thought to improve the quality of life. What a miracle laughter is. No wonder we all crave it.

Solomon stated in Proverbs 17:22, "A cheerful heart is good medicine, but a broken spirit saps a person's strength." Laughing is like medicine for your soul.

We all want to bring laughter and happiness to others, and we all want to receive those things from others. Be a person who helps others laugh, bringing happiness and hope. Help people see the good things in life, especially when circumstances are tough.

Life is short. Enjoy the good things together, work through the bad things together, and keep your humor through it all. Find a person you can laugh with.

---

3   "Humor Therapy: Topic Overview," WebMD, http://www.webmd.com/mental-health/tc/humor-therapy-topic-overview.

CHAPTER 9

BAIT #3: BE YOURSELF

Couples who grow old together change together. Life will change you. People will change you. Circumstances will change you. But there is a core to who you are that remains the same throughout your life.

When it comes to the fundamentals—like a belief system, wanting children or not, agreeing to remain faithful, and how to spend or save money—couples need to be on the same page. Prior to marriage, discuss your hot topics and explain where you stand on them.

But first, get to know who God created you to be. Finding out who you are takes time and requires you to ask yourself difficult questions. It also means getting God's input on those foundational elements of your life.

Knowing yourself, liking yourself, and being yourself are of utmost importance when choosing someone to spend the rest of your life with. If you're never satisfied with the guys you attract, maybe there are some characteristics and expectations you need to deal with.

Regarding surface-level aspects of your personality, likes and dislikes, and preferences, you can decide how much you're willing to alter in order to snag the right man. Ultimately, when you know who you are, you can determine where and how you want to change.

For example, let's say you know you're shy and insecure, especially around new people. So you've remained a wallflower, rarely meeting anyone new. You've already accomplished step one: you know yourself. Step two is figuring out how to become a better conversationalist without completely changing yourself. You will probably always be shy. But you can watch the behavior of good conversationalists—listen to the questions they ask others, observe their gestures and responses, and pick up on those social cues. Step three is practicing what you learned.

KNOWING YOURSELF, LIKING YOURSELF, AND BEING YOURSELF ARE OF UTMOST IMPORTANCE WHEN CHOOSING SOMEONE TO SPEND THE REST OF YOUR LIFE WITH.

If we all loved and accepted ourselves unconditionally, everyone would have confidence and happiness. But usually, we err on one of two opposing sides.

YOU DON'T LIKE THE REAL YOU

When you look at yourself, you see every single flaw, and you magnify those flaws in your mind. Even your strengths look like flaws to you. Since you don't like yourself, you copy other people's personalities to the point where you don't even know your own anymore.

Or if you want to escape your past enough, you'll do everything in your power to forget where you came from.

You become whatever the guy you're dating wants you to be. You go from relationship to relationship never knowing who you really are. You attract men who like controlling your behavior: what you wear, what you look like, what your interests and hobbies are, even who you talk to. And you settle for a guy who treats you like trash.

Later in life, you have to go through an extensive healing process in order to relearn who you are.

Who you are is beautiful. You have an individual personality and you are created in the image of God (Genesis 1:27).

Regardless of what weaknesses you think you have, you don't have to copy every aspect of a person you see as a role model. Embrace your uniqueness, your flaws, and your strengths.

Get counseling if necessary and surround yourself with cheerleaders. Make a list of your strengths and capitalize on them. Find a job you flourish in and compliment yourself daily by verbalizing what your talents are and how they positively impact others. Eventually, you will be able to love yourself and accept yourself for who you really are.

YOU HAVE AN INFLATED VIEW OF YOURSELF

On the opposite side of the spectrum is the girl who won't budge in her likes and dislikes just to get a guy's attention. She won't alter her looks, her interests, or her hobbies. She is who she is and she won't change for anyone.

But there's a reason you're still single, and it's not because every guy out there is a dumb, ugly jerk.

You wait for a man to come along who is equal to your greatness. But there's a reason you're still single, and it's not because every guy out there is a dumb, ugly jerk. It's actually because your attitude comes across as prideful and disinterested.

Instead of truly accepting yourself, you're accepting an inflated view of yourself. You gloss over flaws. You think you're better than others. Because you're the best, you think you deserve the best. With this mentality, you will never change.

But with humility comes a willingness to make compromises. If there's some quirky thing you do that the guy you're with can't stand, you might want to try to change it. After all, you'll want him to adjust some things along the way for you.

The Real You Attracts the Right Person (Eventually)

It's ridiculous to imagine the worm on the end of a hook chasing after a fish. If the fish is curious enough, it will bite.

If you still haven't caught a particular fish you've had your eye on, that's okay! The real you is good enough bait. But if you don't believe that, you'll resort to manipulation.

Deceiving a man in order to lure him in will only end in disaster. You deserve a guy who likes the real you, not a fake you that you've contrived in order to manipulate a man into liking you.

Imagine if a woman communicated her desire for children prior to marriage because the man she was with couldn't wait to be a dad, but two years into the marriage she admits she doesn't want kids. Her spouse will feel betrayed and find it difficult to trust or respect her again.

People create a facade, knowingly or unknowingly, because they want to fit in and be liked. But when you project an image that isn't true to you, you draw people in who may not connect well with you.

The only way you can be fully open with others, especially the opposite sex, is when you love yourself. God is love, and He can show you how to forgive yourself, how to view yourself as beautiful and worthy, and how to like yourself despite your flaws and insecurities.

BUT WHEN YOU PROJECT AN IMAGE THAT ISN'T TRUE TO YOU, YOU DRAW PEOPLE IN WHO MAY NOT CONNECT WELL WITH YOU.

This healthy self-love allows you to remain confident even if you aren't what your fantasy man is looking for. It helps you be realistic with your standards for a spouse because you won't need a man to boost your ego or make you feel worthy or loved. And it brings you back to the author of love, God Himself, who then fills you up with more love.

PART FOUR

NOW WHAT?

In this last section, you'll gain insight as to why it's important to discover God's purpose for you, and how enduring in prayer is the only way to keep God at the center of your search.

You may also discover why you're still single!

CHAPTER 10

THE SHAME GAME

Well-meaning people used to tell me that dating should be fun. I was convinced the reason they thought this was that they hadn't dated in decades.

Dating felt burdensome for me. A weight of anxiety lifted when I got married. Anxiety caused by the expectation to go on dates, meet new people, and get to know guys I was interested in, as well as trying to figure out *Do I like him? Does he like me? Are we a good fit? Is he the right one?*

Being single can be discouraging and exhausting. And women often feel shame from being single, as if they're not respected by their church or society. Sometimes that feeling is contrived from their own thoughts of unworthiness; other times, it's a result of judgments made by friends and family.

Paul says in 1 Corinthians 7:34–35:

> A woman who is no longer married or has never been married can be devoted to the Lord and holy in body and in spirit. But a married woman has to think about her earthly responsibilities and how to please

> her husband. I am saying this for your ben-
> efit, not to place restrictions on you. I want
> you to do whatever will help you serve the
> Lord best, with as few distractions as pos-
> sible.

According to Paul, marriage is a distraction that keeps people from being 100 percent devoted to God. Unfortunately, that knowledge doesn't give many singles a sense of happiness. They still tend to feel shame and/or embarrassment, especially as they age.

However, women can be fulfilled outside of a romantic relationship. They can walk in the purposes God has for them. They can give devoted attention to the work of God.

But that doesn't mean they want to remain single. Knowing there is purpose in their season of singleness doesn't always provide them with contentment.

How can you enjoy life if you desperately want to be married? Here are four ways you can find fulfillment in your singleness and actually enjoy it.

1. Increase Your Faith for Marriage

There is no need to feel shame, embarrassment, or inferiority because you don't have a man by your side. If you have loved ones who cause you to feel ashamed because you're single, don't let those negative voices settle in your heart. Spend more time with people who believe in you and support you. Having the right people around you will help you remain hopeful and happy.

When I was single, I felt like others were more worried about my marital status than I was. But I didn't let their concern affect my faith.

Tell yourself, out loud, that God has a man who is a perfect fit for you. Practice faith thoughts by memorizing Bible verses to encourage yourself. Start with these:

> Jeremiah 29:11 (NIV): "For I know the plans I have for you," declares the Lord, "plans to prosper you and not to harm you, plans to give you hope and a future."

> Psalm 37:4: Take delight in the Lord, and he will give you your heart's desires.

> Proverbs 3:5–6: Trust in the Lord with all your heart; do not depend on your own understanding. Seek his will in all you do, and he will show you which path to take.

> Matthew 6:33: Seek the Kingdom of God above all else, and live righteously, and he will give you everything you need.

> Hebrews 11:1, 6: Faith shows the reality of what we hope for; it is the evidence of things we cannot see. And it is impossible to please God without faith. Anyone who wants to come to him must believe that God exists and that he rewards those who sincerely seek him.

Doubt is easy. Choosing to remain faith-filled is harder. But when you believe you'll find the love of your life, you'll expect great things. You won't feel sorry for yourself, and you'll experience genuine happiness as a single woman.

2. ACCEPT THE FACT THAT YOU'VE GOT ISSUES

Everyone has issues. You do, and so does the person you'll end up marrying.

The men out there who want a girl with no problems aren't for you. They probably haven't accepted the fact that they've got baggage too.

Just because you have "issues," that doesn't mean there's something wrong with you. That way of thinking will only make you depressed. You are a work in progress, and you should give yourself a little grace.

God is constantly healing you, if you're seeking that healing. But you may not solve every problem before you get married. The same is true for your potential spouse.

Let God's standards guide you. What issues are you okay partnering with? And what aren't you okay with?

Is the man you're attracted to addicted to drugs? Is he a felon? Is he an abuser? Be wary. Don't try to be your boyfriend's therapist or savior. You will be sorely disappointed.

Too many women marry guys who cheat, are mean, are too immature to communicate well, and become distant, uninvolved husbands. A woman should have standards in place and wait for a quality man who loves Jesus, loves and respects her, and will be a wonderful companion and father.

Finding the balance between accepting an imperfect man with issues and dismissing a man with unacceptable issues can be difficult. Seek wise counsel from married friends and mentors to glean from their experience. Find out what mistakes they made. Ask them what they think is truly important in a marriage and what isn't. They will have insight as to what issues they thought were big deals prior to marriage but turned out to be nothing. They will also provide an objective perspective to help you see red flags that you may be overlooking.

3. STOP IDOLIZING MARRIAGE

If you don't feel complete without marriage, you won't feel complete after marriage.

Women who idolize marriage think everything will be better once they're hitched. They think a man will rescue them from their unhappiness. They think his role is to make life easier for them.

> # IF YOU DON'T FEEL COMPLETE WITHOUT MARRIAGE, YOU WON'T FEEL COMPLETE AFTER MARRIAGE.

It's normal to crave a life partner who offers companionship and love. But most of the time, the benefits a single person imagines she'll get in marriage are exaggerated. Her husband may not always be able to take care of the cars, the house, the lawn, and the garbage, or always be there to defend her when she needs it. He may have a hectic work schedule that will mean she has to manage the things she always expected a husband would take care of.

If you live in a constant state of "Life will be better when I'm married," you've put marriage on a pedestal. You've created an idol.

Believing that marriage will be your source of happiness, fulfillment, and self-worth can cause a single girl to be envious of married women. She then becomes bitter. She feels like a victim because she can't control her circumstances and find that perfect man. Eventually, she begins blaming others for her unhappiness. She feels depressed and hopeless the longer her dream is delayed. And she won't be happy with anyone she doesn't think is capable of giving her that fantasy.

IF YOU LIVE IN A CONSTANT STATE OF "LIFE WILL BE BETTER WHEN I'M MARRIED," YOU'VE PUT MARRIAGE ON A PEDESTAL.

Don't wait for the perfect man to make life better for you. That mind-set isn't attractive to anyone, especially to a God-fearing man. He knows he won't be able to give you the life you're dreaming about.

Marriage is a beautiful partnership between two people. It is fulfilling and amazing and incredible and exciting. But it won't meet all of your expectations.

God must be in His rightful place in order for you to have a healthy perspective of marriage. God is the fulfiller of your dreams. Worship Him, not the fantasy.

4. Find Your Purpose in God

You want a life full of laughter, family, fulfillment, and overcoming hurdles with loved ones by your side. You feel called to find a man to fall in love with and marry and have children with. But you haven't met the right person yet, and you aren't the type to compromise.

You believe your dreams will come to pass, but since they haven't yet, you wonder what to do in the meantime.

God has a purpose for every season of life you're in. Even the seasons you don't like.

If you think you can't be truly fulfilled until God brings you a husband, you're wrong.

A man, a career, or possessions, do not bring purpose—God does. It's not fair to put that kind of expectation on your future husband. It's not his responsibility.

When you do marry, your satisfaction will dwindle as soon as the honeymoon stage ends. You'll think something is wrong with your husband, your marriage, or you.

So what is God's vision for you in your current season? Ask Him to reveal to you what you are called to right now. Create goals, work toward accomplishing them, and busy yourself with the work of God as Paul discusses in 1 Corinthians 7:34.

This will help you focus on God in all seasons of life. Then you will always be able to find happiness and fulfillment.

CHAPTER 11

WHATEVER YOU LOOSE ON EARTH IS LOOSED IN HEAVEN

Sean liked me for about eight months before we began dating. We had a discussion about dating twice during that time, and both times I let him know I wasn't interested. I was content to remain just friends.

After our second conversation about dating, I walked away thinking, *Watch—I'll probably start liking him.*

Yet he walked away from that conversation ready to move on. He needed to become emotionally disconnected from me, so he began praying that God would either change his heart or change my heart.

At the same time, I began asking God to loose marriage in my life. I wasn't praying specifically for Sean, but on a daily basis I was building my faith. I believed what Jesus said in Matthew 18:18 (NIV), "Truly I tell you, whatever you bind on earth will be bound in heaven, and whatever you loose on earth will be loosed in heaven." I trusted that all the power and authority of heaven was behind my prayer.

The premonition I had after our second conversation became a reality. I started liking Sean. I believe God turned my heart toward him because both of us were praying at the same time. Without realizing it, we were interceding for each other in regard to marriage.

Without God's intervention, I don't know if I would ever have viewed Sean as more than a friend.

In today's generation, marriage requires breakthrough, and breakthrough requires prayer. Lots of it.

But many women dismiss marriage as a topic worthy of prayer because they are content being single. They say, "I trust God. It'll happen when it happens." Or, "I know God's timing is perfect, so I'm not worried."

It's great that you trust God and are at ease with your singleness. But just because you have faith in God for marriage, that doesn't mean you shouldn't fervently seek Him in prayer and do everything you can to see marriage come to pass in your life … if that's His will for you.

BUT POWERFUL FAITH DOESN'T CAUSE US TO CEASE PRAYING. IT PROPELS US TO PRAY.

If you believe that marriage is completely out of your control, you may believe that your prayers won't make a difference. So you aren't motivated to storm the gates of heaven. You sit back, relax, and wait for God to do something.

But powerful faith doesn't cause us to cease praying. It propels us to pray.

If you didn't have a job or any financial support, you would acknowledge that you are in a desperate situation that requires God's help. You may have faith that God will provide you with the right job at the right time. After all,

God won't leave you to starve. But you still do everything you can to get a job. You apply for positions you qualify for. Maybe you go to school to gain more or different skills. You might even take a job you don't really want in order to get by until you find the job you do want. You pray, and maybe fast. And you ask friends for prayer.

There may be multiple jobs for you, but there is only one man you will ultimately choose. So how much more should you be praying for that man than for a job?

Let your prayers begin now. Don't let more years go by before you start to worry. Compel God to action with your prayers.

Take the authority God has given you to loose marriage for yourself in the name of Jesus Christ. Come to Him in strong, enduring faith and watch Him act on your behalf.

DESPERATION AND CONTENTMENT CAN COEXIST

It's painful to have our longings go unfulfilled. The longer this happens, the more convinced we become that God is distant or that He doesn't care. We get comfortable with life the way it is, and we can forget about our dreams. It can be exhausting to fight for something daily in prayer, so we come to accept our singleness.

You can enjoy being single and be comfortable in it, but don't be so proud that you won't even acknowledge your longing for marriage. If you never admit to it, you won't endure in prayer for it, and you may never see that desire fulfilled.

Being content doesn't mean you never long for something you don't have. Being at peace with where you are doesn't mean you can't be desperate for a prayer to be answered.

Paul said he had learned to be content with little and with much (Philippians 4:10–13). But that doesn't mean he didn't dream for more.

We can be content without marriage yet desperately seek God for it. In fact, as you seek God, your faith will be strengthened.

When I was in my early twenties, I heard a pastor at a conference talk about the importance of fasting for breakthrough. He specifically brought up the idea of fasting for marriage. I decided to apply that to my life. Thus began a long journey of fasting and praying.

YOU CAN ENJOY BEING SINGLE AND BE COMFORTABLE IN IT, BUT DON'T BE SO PROUD THAT YOU WON'T EVEN ACKNOWLEDGE YOUR LONGING FOR MARRIAGE.

I thought I was fasting for God to bring the right man into my life. But the breakthrough took place inside me. I was changed, not my circumstances.

I became better able to deal with and overcome my fears regarding marriage. Only then could I respond to God when He allowed me to see Sean the way He saw him. God approved of him for me. But because I was filtering primarily through the lens of societal standards, I wasn't able to see what God saw in him.

I genuinely believed it would require a miracle for God to bring the right man into my life and for me to respond to him. I had become desperate for marriage, even while remaining happy in my singleness.

Some people think that if they truly have faith, they should never exhibit signs of desperation, frustration, doubt, anger, or impatience. But we're not perfect. And we can't hide the fact that we're human from God. So don't pretend your emotions don't exist. God can handle them.

In Luke 18, a widow came before a judge, asking for justice. The judge was so annoyed and worn out by her persistent requests that he finally gave her what she wanted.

How much more is God willing to give you the desires of your heart? Unlike the judge in the story, He loves you deeply and isn't annoyed by your requests. He wants to answer your prayers.

But sometimes God responds to our prayers in unexpected ways. So be open to His answer, even if it's different from what you thought it would be.

When we pray, God often deals with us first, rather than the situation. The fears, baggage, pain, and insecurities we bring into a relationship make finding the right spouse difficult. We can't escape ourselves. So we have to bring God into the picture and allow Him to speak to us.

Let your desire for marriage propel you toward God, and don't give up fighting for it. Come to Him in faith. Seek Him and ask for His miraculous provision. Rely on His grace to get you through. Because He is sufficient.

CHAPTER 12

WHY AREN'T YOU MARRIED YET?

Love is a mystery. In Proverbs 30:18–19 Solomon says, "There are three things that amaze me—no, four things that I don't understand: how an eagle glides through the sky, how a snake slithers on a rock, how a ship navigates the ocean, how a man loves a woman."

Science can explain how an eagle flies, how a snake slithers, and how a ship navigates the ocean, but we have yet to fully understand how a man loves a woman.

The love between God and humankind is surely a mystery, as is the love between a man and a woman. How and why do we fall in love with the people we do? How do we know if it's "true love"? How do we know we won't fall "out" of love? What does love feel like?

Or how about a more personal question: why aren't you married yet? You're taking practical steps to find your spouse. Why don't they seem to be working?

Proverbs 2:2–4 says, "Tune your ears to wisdom, and concentrate on understanding. Cry out for insight, and ask for understanding. Search for them as you would silver; seek them like hidden treasures." Proverbs 25:2 (NIV) says, "It is the glory of God to conceal a matter; to search out a matter is the glory of kings."

When a heartfelt prayer isn't being answered, "search out" the matter and seek understanding from God.

Let's say I withdrew five thousand dollars from my bank account. I kept those hundred-dollar bills in my wallet for a couple of days, during which time I ran errands, went out to lunch, visited friends, and drove to work. When I needed the money, I opened my wallet and discovered the cash was missing.

WHEN A HEARTFELT PRAYER ISN'T BEING ANSWERED, "SEARCH OUT" THE MATTER AND SEEK UNDERSTANDING FROM GOD.

You'd better believe I would retrace my steps. And ask people to help me remember where I had gone during those couple of days. I would drive down every street I had taken. And I would ask God to help me remember what I did. I wouldn't stop my search until I found that money.

If you believe God wants you to be married, follow King Solomon's advice and seek God for understanding and insight as if you were searching for gold and silver. This will bring you clarity and help you figure out why you aren't married yet.

Let's examine some possible reasons you're still single. These applied to me, so maybe you'll relate to them too. These aren't the only reasons, but they're a good place to start.

1. You aren't attracting anyone.
2. You're attracting people you aren't interested in.
3. Now isn't the right time for dating and marriage.
4. You haven't found the right person yet.

Let's look at these individually.

1. YOU AREN'T ATTRACTING ANYONE

Many women go through seasons when they're never asked out. Most women assume that if they have no pursuers, no one is interested. But it's possible that you *are* attracting men, they just aren't asking you out. If that's the case, the fault lies with them, not you.

But we can't control the behavior of others. We can only control our own behavior. We can accept our season of singleness and figure out how to move beyond it.

To help you do that, I've compiled a list of possible reasons you may not be attracting anyone.

You're Too Busy

Your job, your family, your travels may be taking up too much of your time. You simply don't have the capacity to build on your current friendships or make new friends.

If that's the case, getting married is clearly not a top priority for you. If don't believe me, take at look at where you spend your time. If you're never in situations that allow you to meet new people, you must be hoping for a miracle to fall into your lap. You believe people who tell you it'll happen when you least expect it. Unfortunately, this is rarely true.

WE ALL MAKE TIME FOR WHATEVER IS A HIGH PRIORITY TO US.

If you want a promotion, you work harder, you go to networking events, you familiarize yourself with the desired position, and you take the necessary steps to prepare yourself for that next level. But people who say they want a spouse can come up with all kinds of excuses for not making an effort to meet people of the opposite sex.

Maybe you're a homebody. But do you want to get married or not? Crying, binge-watching TV, sipping wine, and venting with friends may help you deal with your loneliness, but they won't get you a spouse. So wipe your tears, get off the couch, and go out and meet some people. We all make time for whatever is a high priority to us.

You're Giving the Wrong Vibe

Do you come across as indifferent or cold around men? Do you give off an attitude that says, *I hate all men*, or, *I'm better than all y'all*, or *You're ugly*?

Don't let apathy or the fear of rejection paralyze you. This vibe says, "You have to work really hard to get me!" And the guy is wondering, *Why?* What is it he's chasing after? A girl who is sure to reject him?

Most men will feel intimidated by women like this, and it's not because of how successful or beautiful they are. It's because of the vibe they're giving. Men are drawn instead to women who make them feel comfortable and accepted.

MOST MEN WILL FEEL INTIMIDATED BY WOMEN LIKE THIS, AND IT'S NOT BECAUSE OF HOW SUCCESSFUL OR BEAUTIFUL THEY ARE.

Change the vibe you're giving out. Give the guy you like hope that you'll say yes to him. Lock eyes with him, smile, and if given the opportunity, sit next to him. Each little step of initiation and response can make a huge impact on your dating life.

Your Heart Is a Prisoner

Women who have been single for a long time learn to protect their hearts from disappointment and pain. They rarely open up to a man. Their hearts may be protected, but they can only offer surface-level emotional availability.

Men are rarely attracted to a woman who seems emotionless. If she never lets him in, he'll eventually move on.

So learn to be vulnerable. Risk the possibility of getting hurt, but hope for the best. The only way you can find this balance is to go into a relationship open-handed. Have the mentality that if it works out, great, but if not, then no big deal. Keep your expectations in check. If you only expect to find a friend, you won't be crushed if the new friendship doesn't turn into a promising romantic relationship.

This will make you appear approachable and attractive, ultimately making it easier for you to find a spouse. When you let your guard down, men will get to know you for who you really are.

You Don't Know How to Accentuate the Real You

Some girls never get asked out because they're waiting around for a man to pursue them, but they don't give him a reason to. They don't have any pursuers because they don't know how to accentuate who they really are.

Take a good look at yourself and ask, "What type of person will I most likely attract based on my appearance?" Are you okay with the answer? If so, great. If not, start taking better care of yourself physically. For example, if your looks can be accentuated with makeup, wear some. Choose a hairstyle that compliments you and clothing that looks good on your body.

If you want someone to notice your great personality, show it off! Don't wait around for a guy to solve the mystery of who you are. Make it easier for him by talking about things you're interested in, asking questions, and discussing work or hobbies or goals.

You're Stuck in Your Surroundings

Another reason you may not be attracting anyone is that you're limited to your surroundings. The majority of your friends are already married or dating, and you live in a small town with few prospects.

I'm from a small town, and in one year fourteen of my friends married each other. A few years later, I moved to Seattle—not to get married, but to move on with my life. And there I met Sean. I'm not suggesting you move just to find a spouse. But if you haven't met the man of your dreams where you are, you might gain a lot by moving. It could be an incredible life change for you in many ways.

If moving isn't an option, you'll have to rely on friends from different cities to set you up on blind dates. Or consider online dating. Create an online profile and see what happens.

2. You're Attracting People You Aren't Interested In

Reevaluate the kind of man you think you're compatible with. Ask yourself why you aren't attracted to the people who are attracted to you. Dig deep and try to understand the real reasons.

Is it because all of them lack qualities that are deal breakers for you? Are those the standards God has given you or requirements you've contrived?

Are you afraid of commitment? Do you think you're better than they are? Are you nitpicky? Is marriage not really important to you right now? Are you afraid of failure? Does it seem easier to remain single than to figure out how to make a relationship work?

If you aren't in a relationship even though you have pursuers, ask yourself what needs to change. It's possible you're the one keeping yourself single. After all, you are the common denominator.

Though it's important to analyze yourself so you can get revelation on what areas, if any, need to change, know that there is an extremely low number of men who are right for you. Someday you'll marry your One and Only, but until then, you'll have a consistent stream of eligible bachelors crossing your path who are all wrong for you.

The only way to find out which man is the right one is to keep God at the center of your search, asking Him for wisdom and discernment, and to give guys a chance even if you aren't initially attracted to them.

3. NOT THE RIGHT TIME, NOT THE RIGHT PERSON

The answer most women give to the question of why they aren't married yet is that it's not the right time or they haven't met the right person. If you've been praying daily, you've adjusted your standards, you've become open to different types of men, you've dealt with your issues, and you're still not married, you may be right with that conclusion.

You have a destiny from God, and I believe your desires will lead you to that destiny. But if you aren't married yet, remember that God's ways are higher than ours (Isaiah 55:9). When we put God in charge, He'll do what He wants when He wants and how He wants.

He puts the puzzle pieces of our lives together. He sees the big picture. He has our best interests in mind. He knows us better than we know ourselves. He knows the type of spouse you need better than you do. He understands your insecurities and your weaknesses, and He wants to bring strengths to you in the person you marry.

Spend significant time asking God to provide you with the person He wants you to spend the rest of your life with. If we submit our lives to God, He will work out all things for good (Romans 8:28). He is on your side. He will not leave you or forsake you (Deuteronomy 31:6).

God looks at each of us as an individual. He isn't comparing you or your progress (or lack thereof) to others. So why are you? We always feel unfairly treated when we compare ourselves to someone else.

If God gives something to someone else before you, what does that matter? If He answers someone else's prayer before He answers yours, so what?

Let's take a look at some people in the Bible who went through a similar waiting period that you're going through. We can follow their examples of fervently seeking God's promises.

In Luke 8, we read about a woman who had been bleeding for twelve years. She finally had the chance to touch the hem of Jesus' clothes in hopes of getting healed. When she did, Jesus said, "Someone touched me; I know that power has gone out from me" (8:46 NIV). She persistently prayed, and she was finally healed.

In 1 Samuel 1, we read about a barren woman named Hannah, who, in her "deep anguish," asked God for a child (1:10–11 NIV). The priest got so tired of her apparent drunkenness that he confronted her. She explained her behavior. Once he understood her story, he prophesied that a child would be born to her. The following year she gave birth to a son.

In Genesis 26, we read about Abraham, who was told by God that he would have descendants as numerous as the stars. He had no child and was too old to conceive. But after prayer, and tested faith and patience, God gave him that child.

Why did that woman have to bleed for twelve years before Jesus healed her? Why did it take God years to give Hannah the child she wanted, even though her husband's other wife already had children? Why did Abraham have to wait twenty years after God promised him a child?

We don't know for sure. God does teach us patience in times of tribulation. And there are some issues that need time to heal. We can learn and grow in the waiting season of life.

But those things are of little comfort. After all, other people are getting married—people with issues, people less attractive than you, people who could benefit more from a longer waiting period. Why are you different?

You aren't. Your job is to trust Him, believe, never give up or lose hope, and continue to take advantage of Jesus opportunities, like the woman with the issue of blood. Seek God's face, like Hannah did. And have enduring faith, like Abraham did.

These people received their promises. You too can receive yours.

Made in the USA
Las Vegas, NV
02 August 2022

52590685R00094